SUPERSIZING bliss

How we have betrayed our homes and the happiness we seek

TOBY WITTE

SPARK Publications
Charlotte, North Carolina

Supersizing Bliss
How We Have Betrayed Our Homes and the Happiness We Seek
Toby Witte

Designed, produced, and published
by SPARK Publications
SPARKpublications.com
Charlotte, North Carolina

Printed in the United States of America
Hardback, April 2023, ISBN: 978-1-953555-47-2
Library of Congress Control Number: 2023901090

Dedication

To Liz.
My Happiness.

"On a quest to find the true definition of home and how the houses in which we live might contribute directly to the health and happiness of their occupants, Toby Witte explores the individual elements of architectural design and presents an alternative blueprint for changing the way we build single family homes in America."

Mark R. LePage, AIA, NCARB
Founder of EntreArchitect

"The flight from intimacy in residential design betrays our need to have houses create calm, reduce stress, and insulate us from the outside world. Witte challenges rising expectations and champions what's possible in reasonably-sized spaces."

George Smart, HAIA
Founder of USModernist

"Witte excavates desire with a sincerity that is the sexiest stalwart of design. He doesn't merely appease. He psychically sketches, etches, and constructs the metaphorical and enveloping chaise lounge where his clients would choose to languish...forever."

John W. Love, Jr.
Interdisciplinary Artist | Guggenheim Fellow

"I'm twenty years into my journey as a residential architect and Supersizing Bliss gave me a new framework for identifying what matters."

"Toby is like that great teacher who makes complex ideas simple. Supersizing Bliss is a must-read for future homeowners and their architects!"

Kyle Barke, AIA, NCARB
Architect | Founder and Principal of Primary Projects

"Architects often write for other architects, but Supersizing Bliss is devoted to architecture's inhabitants. Witte's book offers insights into many of the little-known frustrations, desires, and dreams architects have for the built environment. The accessible book is a kind of annotated love letter to architecture, written by an architect, to all occupants of houses."

Blaine Brownell, FAIA, LEED AP
Professor and Director, David R. Ravin
School of Architecture, University of North Carolina

"An array of
hitherto ignored
materials and
forms could reveal
their qualities
while the status
quo would
be prevented
from coercively
suggesting itself
to be the natural
and eternal order
of things."

—————————————————

*—Alain de Botton in The
Architecture of Happiness*

"We shape our buildings and afterwards our buildings shape us."

—*Winston Churchill*

Table
of Contents

Introduction

A Word of Caution

As a disclaimer, I should say the words on these pages are meant for a specifically North American audience. But without doubt some generalities might be applicable the world over.

It's my intention to lay bare a few of the realities of how our houses have come to be and what you can and should ask for instead in order to create a home that will provide you with lasting happiness.

I hope I will be successful in showing you how a single-family home constitutes a luxury. And if you engage in creating one for yourself, I hope you find the conviction to dive in for the right kind of richness.

Please understand I meant for this collection of thoughts to be read as questions, notions, and starting points for further conversations. I apologize if they sound like opinions. If you look for substantiation of any claims, you will not find them. If I miss addressing your specific pain through my blinding hubris, let me know. I aim to portray just a few realities we face and as they have shown themselves to me personally. Other experts in this field have seen more. Others have done the research and recording. Others have gone deeper and have addressed aspects of my rambling with substance.

I hope to generate some curiosity and break some seals to allow you to create a home that is exceptional and extraordinary, to ultimately allow for more joy in your life. I hope to provide you with a sketch of how to successfully approach the making of the house of your dreams. It is my sincere wish to provide you with an outlook that will enable you to supersize your own personal bliss.

Priming bliss

A brief introduction to the myths and forces that have shaped our houses and some of the richness and qualities we could tap into.

A Sense of Home

We do not have to live in houses. But if we do, we should realize it is a luxury. Let's treat it as one.

Instead of a house, isn't what we really seek a home? We yearn for a moment of pause, a place of safety, a sense of repose. Don't we want to climb into the blanket fort we have long forgotten? To be held in our parents' embrace one more time?

We know how it feels when we shed our day uniform and don the sweatpants, pull up the blanket, grab our comfort food, and lose ourselves in a movie, a book, or a shared drink.

We know when judgments fall and expectations ebb, when nothing is asked of us but to show up, when we are left to be, to find ourselves. We enjoy the freshness of our curiosity after letting go, when we again find the strength to explore.

We want to wake up without haste, to be greeted by the warm rays of the morning's sun, a loving embrace, and the promise of adventures ahead. We want to be allowed to dip our toes into the unknown without fear of hurt or strife. We want to play naked. The innocent probing of our world that our children are experts in is what we want to wallow in. We want to discover. We want to be surrounded by those who love us without conditions. We want to be appreciated and adored for who we are. The person we see ourselves to be is what we want to be encouraged to become.

We ask for a home that can provide the stage for these conditions we seek. We ask for a place that not only allows for these circumstances, but encourages them. We yearn for a built environment that is not only supportive but enriching even intoxicating—a home that tells us we have arrived. We ask for a space that is not only a reflection of our innermost desires and memories, but proves to us the best is still to come.

That is the home we need. That is the home we deserve. That is the home we ought to live in.

Unfortunately, the houses offered to us have failed to step up to the task. It is safe to say only the rarest among us have had the privilege of experiencing a physical surrounding capable of doing all the above. The houses we live in are the furthest from it.

Fig. 1: A cozy reading nook in the Schönberg Residence, 2010, Toby Witte.

If we ask for a house to provide these qualities we so deserve, we need to dig deeper. If we ask for a house to be our home, we need to ask for the specific, the riches that are possible, and the luxuries we crave. Let's have a look.

The Ad

The image made it into the annals of architectural literature. It shows the newest Mercedes-Benz, an 8/38 PS Roadster, parked in front of the most avant-garde and edgy home available. The house is a white modernist box on slender stilts with dark ribbons of glass stretching along the facade alluding to a private interior. Exterior spaces are cutting up the volume underneath and above. The entire scene is an expression of elegance and style. It is cheeky, edgy, and fresh.

The year is 1928. A female beauty, dancer Elsbeth Böklen has a leg scandalously raised on a sideboard and offers a provocative look. Nowadays, she would actually be allowed to drive.

Even today, this house of the Weissenhof Estate has not lost its luster as a modern icon. It still raises eyebrows. Designed by Le Corbusier and built a year earlier for the architectural exhibition of the Deutscher Werkbund in Stuttgart, the house helped push the Modern style onto the world's scene.

Fig. 2: Mercedes-Benz 8/38 PS Roadster in front of the Le Corbusier House at Stuttgart's Weissenhof Estate, 1928.

The car, on the other hand, is dated, to say the least. From the perspective of a century later, it looks like a carriage missing its horse.

What happened? Cars these days resemble spaceships. Women are not only allowed to drive, they may even own a car, if you can just imagine. They can own it without a husband. Times have changed. But the houses sold to us look as if they have progressed very little.

Mercedes-Benz still takes the same picture for their advertising. The cars are sleeker. The houses are not.

And if we look around us, the houses sold to us today have actually regressed. They try to resemble aristocratic French country houses from a time when cars didn't even exist—a time when buggies had horses.

It should leave us to wonder what we are missing out on with the houses we live in.

» And if we look around us, the houses sold to us today have actually regressed. They try to resemble aristocratic French country houses from a time when cars didn't even exist—a time when buggies had horses. «

The Luxury of Excess

_____

Before we begin, we have to spend a moment and discredit single-family houses and understand them for the aberrations they actually are. The sooner I tell you the truth, the sooner you can consider how to do them right, if you decide to do them at all.

If we were to respond honestly to the environmental challenges we are facing from the perspective of housing, we would decide to live in mixed-use and multifamily co-op buildings within midsize compact cities. The smarter choice would be multistory buildings that house a number of apartments, offices, and ground-level retail spaces alike.

If we were to address the often-cited housing crises intelligently, we would opt for the same kind of compact urban surroundings. Instead of continuing to suggest a superfluousness of single-family residences, these multiunit complexes could be co-owned by their inhabitants or rented out by its owners.

If we were to do this, we could actually afford to be housed. We could provide one roof for a handful of households and not just one. We could consider one foundation for all, not one for each house. The math is easy. There wouldn't be any driveways and long runs of utilities for a single-use house. Instead, we would offer shared modes of transportation and shorter distances for our roads. The savings would multiply.

In doing so, we would also enjoy the kind of vibrant, multicultural places of opportunities and interaction that tickle our need for culture and community. Compact tapestries of life could enrich us within animated urban centers.

Then we might even have the chance to notice each other. We might be able to meet and be given the chance to understand each other's struggles and joys. We might have an opportunity to face our inequities and commonalities.

Picture a city, if you will, with a tight network of state-of-the-art public transportation. Picture the grocery store, bakery, and cafe underneath the ten-story building that holds your apartment, your home. You can reach your place of work without a car and within a short commute. The same goes for cultural events and institutions. There would be a farmers market on your street every Thursday and a street festival once a month.

The architecture to provide the stage for this, as well as the infrastructure, is compact. It is shared. It has thus less negative impact on our environment than the endless sea of our suburban housing sprawl.

In order to create a viable built environment that is not destroying our habitat, we have to build smarter. We have to use far less carbon fuel and produce less carbon dioxide and even reclaim some of it. We have to use renewable resources and sources of energy.

Single-family houses, in general, do quite the opposite. They are by default more wasteful in their creation, their operation, their maintenance, and their inclusion in our infrastructure.

Obnoxious as such, single-family houses manhandle themselves into being a luxury. To become as viable ecologically as a more compact living arrangement, they have to work that much harder to be successfully created and run. In order not to be environmentally more destructive, single-family residences are by default less economical.

As homesteads, single-family houses tend to one person, a couple, or one family and ignore

Fig. 3: Vibrant downtown scene in Asheville, North Carolina.

our need for community, social engagement, and a cultural connection. Their extraction of the one unit of housing from the rest, their singling out, makes them a folly. They are a token of our undeniable narcissistic needs, our desire to be special, to be tended to, to be heard, and to be seen.

Once we can admit as much, we might be able to agree we are truly creating and choosing them over more sensible options for the pure unadulterated pampering of ourselves, for the luxury of a man-made environment that tends to our singular way of life, for our personal luxury of being.

Let's admit to that. Let's own up to it. It is perfectly permissible to allow ourselves to indulge in the wasteful whimsies single-family residences are. That is, if we understand the pressure points of a culture and industry forcing us to contemplate the useless and discover the potential of doing it right.

When you do, chances are you won't find a bakery within walking distance, but a quietude in its place. There won't be a ten-minute light rail ride to the theater, but maybe an undisturbed and unshared view of the mountain range. There won't be low mortgage payments for the practical flat, but real expenditure for features that are meant for you and you only. There won't be a leaking roof we all share into for repairs, but a bill you alone are responsible for. There won't be literal zero-carbon footprints from your front stoop to the grocery next door, but an immediate and quiet walk in nature.

Single-family houses are a luxury. They are costly. They are asocial. They are impractical. They are nonsensical. They are an answer to the housing needs of only a few, those who are willing and able to admit and pay for the superfluous.

Nonetheless, all of us should be offered spaces that are better designed, lest we accept the mediocre living standards offered by the housing units sold to us, be they single-family houses or apartments, owned or rented.

Let's see if we can appreciate these considerations. Can we separate the qualities of a home from the house as an entity? If we are still asking to create a house, can we approach the task with the appropriate mindset and expectations? Let's see if we can gain a better understanding of how the houses we get to choose from or the precedents for our own creation come to be.

And let's see if we can find an appreciation for qualities of space that can be applied to all physical forms of living, including townhomes, cohousing, or mixed-use buildings.

However, we will continue to look at the single-family residence here specifically.

The Kit

At the same time as that image of the Mercedes was taken almost a century ago, you could buy a house plan and kit of construction materials from Sears stateside. Or you could browse one of many "Lady Periodicals" such as *Good Housekeeping, Ladies' Home Journal, The Household Magazine, Modern Priscilla,* and *Woman's Home Companion.* And if that still did not do it, plan books proliferated with ever-repeating house plans with sparse differences.

Rest assured, you know these houses well. You may happen to live in one. Or maybe your parents do. Or maybe you live in a descendent of these originals, a version but a few years old.

In these houses, the functions are cut up into separate spaces. They have a dining room to eat. For cooking, they provide a kitchen. There is a bedroom for sleeping and for lounging, a living room.

Over the last century nothing much has changed, except you can buy the plans online nowadays and the houses have blown up in size. Other changes are mostly insignificant. The idea of a so-called

THE NORWICH

▲ SEVEN ROOMS, BATH, LAVATORY AND ATTACHED GARAGE

THIS attractive home is the answer to many requests for a compact Colonial type with attached garage. This picturesque home makes an instant appeal to all who see it. The architect has ingeniously utilized every bit of available space to provide seven rooms, bath, lavatory and two-car garage of ample proportions and at low cost.

The exterior walls are planned to be covered with wide siding, which when painted white or ivory, forms a pleasing background for dark colored shutters and roof.

The Hooded front entrance is well proportioned and gives protection to the front door.

THE FLOOR PLANS

The first floor plan contains living room, dining room, kitchen, pantry, lavatory and a second living room which is suitable for den or library. Note the attractive porch opening out of the living room.

The second floor plan has three large bedrooms, seven closets, bath and stair hall. Plenty of large windows and good wall space are noticeable.

At the base price quoted we will furnish all materials needed to build this house, consisting of lumber, lath, roof shingles, wide bevel siding, building paper, millwork and 6-panel doors, Colonial back band trim, pine panelling in library, Linoleum for kitchen, bath and lavatory, oak floors in remaining rooms, Elgin Manhattan hardware, enamel for interior trim, varnish for doors and floors, sheet metal and outside paint materials.

You can make your own selection of heating, lighting fixtures and plumbing. Study pages 12 to 15 and fill in blank for complete delivered price.

**MODERN HOME
No. 3342
NOT ALREADY CUT**

FIRST FLOOR PLAN

SECOND FLOOR PLAN

Fig. 4: Modern Homes Catalog, Page 38, The Norwich, 1936, Sears, Roebuck & Co.

open floor plan, for example, has not changed the equation. We just ripped down the wall between the kitchen and the living room. The spaces continue to be individual boxes for each function.

We have added a few cells as well. For a while, we were fine with placing a TV in the living room until we conceived to pair it with a so-called family room. We added a garage and then, so clever was our industrial ingenuity, a bonus room above. In doing so, we essentially began selling the empty attic space on top of our parked cars as something to be desired.

Significant effort went into the packaging of more and more square feet into an idea in itself that was to be coveted. The marketing efforts of developers and house-plan providers went into high gear selling the same plan over and over again, each iteration a copy of the next. None of it reflects how we want to live. Nor are they a reflection of our needs and desires and our life experience—which is, of course, beside the point.

These plans and houses are the result of heartless impersonal companies trying to create something on the cheap and selling it as something we are told to crave.

After they sold house plans and kits to the masses, we realized we can do the same with the houses themselves. You have seen the neighborhoods popping up on the fields around our cities. Chances are, you live in one. Or maybe your parents do.

Henry Ford famously said about the Model T that you could have it in any color as long as it was black. Today you can have any house you wish for as long as it is in builder beige. The image of Charlie Chaplin working away on the assembly line in the movie *Modern Times* comes to mind. That is what these neighborhoods are—assembly lines for mass-produced houses. They are part of a mass industry selling you the idea of home ownership.

It is a concept I would prefer to call "house ownership" because homes they do not offer. To pile a few studs, drywall, and shingles onto a heap does not make a home. A home should be about you and your lifestyle. It should be about your dreams. It should be about the goose bumps you should feel every single day. A home should caress you, envelop you, bring happiness to you.

These houses, though, that are made available to us, are pumped out by the millions with no consideration for our well-being. They are cold carcasses of industrial thrift.

It is highly unlikely they could succeed in providing a home for us. That is not their purpose. They are mere vehicles for business transactions.

» A home should be about you and your lifestyle. It should be about your dreams. It should be about the goose bumps you should feel every single day. A home should caress you, envelop you, bring happiness to you. «

The Mudroom

We walked up to these houses a century ago from the bus, the car, or even the horse-drawn buggy until the car completely took hold of our common consciousness.

It used to be that we walked up to a house as homeowners or guests and entered through the front door. And so we asked these entries to represent our ambitions and the image of ourselves we desired to project.

Now we arrive solely by car and park it in a garage. And we enter the house through the mudroom. We enter from the most to the second most utilitarian space in our house. We enter past the dried-up paint cans, leaking oil canisters, piles of reeking sport paraphernalia, and overflowing recycling bins. That's how our houses greet us.

But we still spend an enormous amount of funds and effort on the representative front door, a front door that often lacks a walkway leading up to it. And why should there be one? We do not use the front door. Even our guests are being ushered in past our unmentionables.

Fig. 5: Inviting entry of the Gerendák Residence accessed from the garage or by foot, 2022, Toby Witte.

Even so, the only remodel to our houses, it turns out, that increases their real estate value is the upgrading of the front entrance. Try to figure that one out. It is absurd.

Instead, we should be welcomed and uplifted when we arrive at our home. After a hard day at work or a high-octane social outing, we should come home to a warm and empathetic welcome. Our homes should beckon us in through an experience immediately suggesting we have arrived, we are safe, and the outside world cannot reach us. We should be surprised by a sublime beauty emanating from the physical environment that envelops us day after day. A beauty that bans all stress, that is uplifting, that is rejuvenating and confirming. We should be welcomed properly to our own sanctuary of bliss. No matter how we arrive.

The entry to our houses we use daily should hint at the glorious happiness we expect to find inside.

>> The entry to our houses we use daily should hint at the glorious happiness we expect to find inside. <<

Two Planes

In 1951, the Farnsworth House was revealed in Plano, Illinois. A modern masterpiece, it took architect Ludwig Mies van der Rohe, director of Berlin's Bauhaus and head of the department of architecture at the Illinois Institute of Technology in Chicago, almost seven years to bring to fruition. It broke with all conventions of the idea of residential living.

Two simple white planes, thin white horizontal steel slabs, hovered over the often-flooded grounds of a secluded nine-acre riverfront property. One plane constituted the floor, the other the roof. The rest was glass. Only a single, room-sized core in the center of this space held a spot for privacy for the inhabitant's unseemly routines.

A third thin white horizontal surface jutted out from underneath to provide additional exterior space and the path into the home. This passage of entry ushered you through the most public moments, from nature to open, semi-open, and enclosed spaces, to ultimately finding rest in an interior lounging area.

This home is said to be blistering hot in the summer and freezing cold in the winter. The slender steel structure has rusted and continued to be threatened by the ever-rising waters. Even though it was conceived to hover over the floods, it has been drowned many times. Mies is said to have had an affair with and was ultimately fired by the owner, Edith Farnswoth. The construction went over budget by 28 percent. And so, one can argue, on many scales, the project was a complete failure.

But as an architectural search for the essence of enclosed space, it remains arguably unparalleled. Mies has been credited with the dictum that "less is more." This structure shows why.

Those planes solely defined the overall spaces. They created a place unburdened by anything superfluous. When sitting in one of his Barcelona chairs in the lounging area, one could appreciate how the exterior became the interior without interruption—a difference delineated only by the edge of the horizontal surfaces.

Structurally, it should be mentioned, Mies achieved this by separating the walls' formal qualities from their structural ones. Slender exterior steel posts hold up the roof. The walls are left to vanish visually and to remain as glass solely for the purpose of climate control.

The areas of lounging, cooking, eating, and sleeping rolled from one to the next. Yet, they were well defined as they settled around the wood-clad core like pearls on a necklace. While the functions were clearly delineated, the spaces borrowed from each other.

The overhead and floor surfaces provided enough definition to let you know you were there. They were enough to create a place, a moment for being.

The materiality of steel, glass, and wood was refined and proposed to be equally suave, machined, and warm.

This house was superbly simple and impressively rich—in texture, the play of light and shadows, the display of the changing seasons, and nature's daily mood swings. It was rich in the qualities with which the spaces were defined and with the intentionality that was not only given to each function, to each moment of occupation, but also to the craft and quality that went into the building of it. We are told Mies asked for the weld lines to be ground down before the painting of the steel.

Fig. 6: An exterior view of the Farnsworth House, 1951, Mies van der Rohe.

This one house reframed the discussion around and the potential for residential dwellings. It created an entirely new paradigm. It provided a radically new answer to what the structure of a home could be reduced to and simultaneously to what magnitude of quality space could be elevated.

If we are talking about providing goose bumps to your daily life, this home did just that.

Some Myths around House Ownership

Since the creation of the Farnsworth House, a mere, yet still grandiose, 1,586 square feet, the average size of houses in the US has grown from 1,100 to far over 2,600 square feet.[1] Yet our families have lost on average one member.[2] In other words, each of us gobbles up three times as much floor area to live in.

That is just us. The stuff we hoard has gone haywire. The average American needs 830 percent[3] more space for storage than Edith Farnworth would have.

House ownership has hung around 65 percent of Americans over the last decade.[4] This means 35 percent of us don't own a house, or more precisely, live in an owned housing unit.

Single-family houses are only slightly above one half of all residences being built.[5] The other half is made up of townhouses, duplexes, apartments, and the like.

Only about 70 percent of children live with both their parents these days. And less than 50 percent of households have a married couple occupying it. Only a third of all households are occupied with a married couple plus children.[6]

Edith Farnsworth, as a single person owning her home, was one of 5 percent. She would now be among 35 percent of our population.[7]

It is safe to say that the white picket fence surrounding the family of four with mom and dad doting over their son and daughter and their tail-wagging pooch is but a pastiche from what we remember a Norman Rockwell painting to be. It is also safe to say that a four- or five-bedroom house is hardly a universally fitting answer to our various forms of household makeup.

We all know we don't use our formal dining rooms anymore, except possibly for two hours on the fourth Thursday in November each year. And if I were to ask you what the drawing room you just purchased is for, you wouldn't be able to tell me.

Presidential administrations ever since Abraham Lincoln signed the 1862 Homestead Act have provided ever new measures to promote the idea of single-family house ownership. We have loaded the idea with pathos and financial superiority. When we own a house, we tell ourselves, we are living the American Dream. When we own a house, we are building up our equity. Not even the financial crash in 2008 taught us any better. The entire world economy was brought to its knees by our houses. The myths and fears of missing out on the idea of owning a single-family house was hyped to the point at which the world's economy was brought to a screeching halt. But by golly, it is the cornerstone of an American identity of self-reliance and individual freedom! It is testimony to our self-reliance. Both the Obama and Trump administrations have thereafter tried to further the ideal, as the two have found different approaches toward the aspect of financial equity by fighting for and against the Affirmatively Furthering Fair Housing rule. The Biden administration was faced with a sudden increase of public awareness about the issue of a racial gap in wealth and home ownership— the very real inequality in the perceived financial equity.

The house means wealth. The house means being an American. With the house, we are part of something greater. And some of us just have to fight that much harder to belong in it.

We have even come to measure the country's economic health by housing starts. The number of new residential construction projects is being released each month by the US Department of Commerce. We eagerly share where the numbers land and rush to the stock market to buy and sell our financial future—partly based on where they fall.

And yet again, whether a single-family house actually makes for an appropriate answer to issues of equality, housing, and building wealth, whether it bears the right measures to combat the climate catastrophe we find ourselves in, or provides useful responses to the question of how we should live, are considerations we blissfully ignore.

Builders Build

———————

Less than 2 percent of all houses involve the work of an architect.[8] And about 75 percent of our construction takes place in the great American seas of urban sprawl surrounding our cities.[9] You can say architects are not involved in creating the places we inhabit.

Yet, architects are uniquely trained to provide innovative new ideas. They harbor treasure troves of creative suggestions about materials, structure, and energy-efficient measures. Architects are trained to create spaces that will make you want to weep for joy. They know how to handle sunlight, the topography of a property, concerns of privacy, and unusual building grounds. They have combed through the tomes of architectural history, studied precedents, and never tire of visiting the newest excesses of their colleagues' fantasies around the world. And some have grown to be masters of their craft—true sculptors of inhabitable art.

The houses you adore in such TV shows as *The World's Most Extraordinary Homes* or on the pages of *Dwell* magazine are conceived from their humble and collective genius. Those designs make up the 2 percent of our houses architects actually get to consider. If you happen to read this in a house you call your own and look around you, chances are the environment you see was not graced by their attention.

In North America, it is primarily builders who create the houses we live in without expert designers involved, most often at the behest of developers. They pump out over one and a half million houses a year in the United States.[10] The name of the game for most of them is to be formulaic, repetitive, and safe. The new, the different, and the specific constitute unknowns. And unknowns are expensive. Developers exist to make money.

There are twenty-two home building companies listed on the New York Stock Exchange. You might have heard such names as Beazer Homes USA, D. R. Horton, KB Home, and the PulteGroup. They are shareholder owned. Who knows, they might even populate your retirement investments. We ask them to make money. That's their job and they better be good at it. What they most likely don't care about are the desires and dreams of the inhabitants of the houses they churn out. The last thing they need is the input of an architect.

And yet we think our houses are meant for us to live in. We believe they are custom made for us and our needs; they are considered and designed for our lives. For the majority, that is not the case.

Even the privately run, smaller builders that care about their craft face the same real estate market and mindset. Except for a few—the good and the brave—they have little choice but to stick to the formulas that have proven safe and cost effective.

As for those few—it is the good builder's métier to build well, to be an expert at all aspects of construction. We cannot ask them to also be the source of good design. In fact, an entire team of specialists might need to be assembled. Besides architects, or residential designers, and builders, it might become necessary to also rely on the guidance of interior designers, landscape architects, energy efficiency experts, structural engineers, civil engineers, and many more.

Fig. 7: Suburban Sprawl, Las Vegas.

Good Design Is Intimate

What, then, should we ask of our homes if we wanted them to actually serve our particular needs and desires? What should we ask for if we could have our home designed from scratch just for us?

We could ask that a home be intimate. If you touched it, if you so much as looked at it, if you walked in it, you should feel some goose bumps.

And how does a home exude such intimacy? Or better yet, how does a home elicit such intimacy from its inhabitants? It may, for instance, lie in its play of scale and its resonance with one's particular story.

Not unlike that of the homeowners-to-be of the Woung House, who hailed from Jamaica with a Chinese heritage and became our clients. They had shared with us their memories of a courtyard wall guiding their path from and to their childhood home.

The transition from the exterior to the interior of a home is always difficult. The change of scale is monumental. You are essentially pushed from a wide-open space with direct access to literally the outer reaches of our solar system and galaxies beyond into a small cramped box topped with a lid and shut off to the world.

As a matter of fact, most of our houses offer this transition through a cutout in a paper-thin outer skin. They are not unlike the empty cardboard box left over from your recent refrigerator purchase a child has transformed into their imagination's dream estate. Three cuts into the side and a door with an operable flap is created. Please glance at your front door and nod in agreement. It's not much different.

For our clients, though, we tried something else. We wedged a vestibule in between two taller, clearly defined, independent volumes of their home. One side was a garage and guest suite, the other the house. The vestibule was defined by a single roof plane that flared up from the front entry porch and main door. Exterior walls were omitted. Only the exterior siding materials of the two buildings on either side were allowed for a vertical demarcation. The front and back were left untouched and only enclosed by glass. Our intention and hope were for the occupants to enter a conditioned space, while seemingly being still outside. As they entered, they would look right back out. We restrained our efforts to provide only a roof to a space that was already defined by two sections of the building, or rather two separate buildings, in and of themselves.

From there, the vestibule opened up to the adjacent spaces by way of a few folds into the two adjoining structures. To round it up, we introduced a gently curved eight-foot-tall exterior masonry wall. Freestanding, it picked up the movement of our clients' approach to their home. It started far out in front of the foyer, greeted them, and gently guided them inside into the half interior, half exterior entry space. The wall was to act as a kind hand, patting them on their shoulder, helping them to find their way inside.

The same masonry wall found itself reincarnated as separate entities, in other parts inside and outside the home, further blurring the lines between the two realms and ever so defining the approach into the more private parts of their home.

The elements (walls, roof plane, and building volumes) and the material palette with different

Fig. 8: Backside of the freestanding wall segments leading into the foyer of the Woung House, 2015, Toby Witte.

tactile qualities (rough textured masonry to cold metal siding and smooth glass) joined, not unlike a symphony, to guide our clients from the wide-open exterior to the contracting and expanding passages and livable spaces. Hopefully, in the process, the front door was not even noticed as a distinct point delineating the crossing of hard border lines.

And hopefully the freestanding wall and its siblings elsewhere in the home equally guided the homeowners' imagination to memories long forgotten and a sense of home, possibly most intense during their childhood years.

Our homes, when they are created by a caring hand and a compassionate eye, might have the chance to be experienced as an act of intimacy. Homes that are not only cognizant of our memories and life story, but are also welcoming to our engagement, will have the chance to become deeply personal affairs.

>> And how does a
home exude such
intimacy? Or better
yet, how does a
home elicit such
intimacy from its
inhabitants? It may,
for instance, lie in
its play of scale
and its resonance
with one's
particular story. <<

McMansions

If you find yourself driving through older single-family neighborhoods of American cities, you might see smaller bungalows, shotgun, mill, or various other traditional houses disappearing and making room for big multistory infill residences. These tend to fill out their property and dwarf their neighbors. Often, they seem to ruin the very quaint neighborhood mood most of us are drawn to in the first place. You might ask yourself, "Why do builders build so big?"

The drivers are two numbers—square feet and the ZIP Code.

Banks finance the majority of houses currently sold. They are, in fact, owned by banks. Another myth to bust is that you are really not a house owner. You are maybe a partial house owner at best. The banks' vehicles of choice are mortgages and construction loans. And if there is the lending of money, there is a real estate appraiser. I should not miss the opportunity to inform you that the etymological origin of the word "mortgage" is a "dead pledge." Go figure.

The financial institutions issue a request for an independent appraisal immediately after you ask for a mortgage. They want to know what the house is worth before they hand out any money. It makes sense. It is not surprising, given the sporadic conservative nature of these institutions, that they prefer measurable metrics. The ubiquitous nature of our suburban landscape comes in handy. If everything is the same, we can compare the particular comfortably with the general. And so it is also not surprising that the appraisal largely measures the two numbers of square feet and ZIP Code. We compare these houses with their size and their location.

If there are plenty of houses around ours that look the same and have been sold for a certain price, then ours should be worth the same. If there is more of that house, then it should be worth proportionally more.

The house owners do not enter the equation, outside of their proof of a sufficient financial background and promising cash flow. They are mere conduits between the banks' and the developers' business. They might be considered as ensured users and free stewards of the banks' investments. The house owners are reduced to cogs in a business transaction without a say in the matter. They are financial backstops, custodians of other people's business interests.

When builders find an empty property in an existing neighborhood surrounded by smaller and much older houses, they are immediately faced with an uphill battle. There isn't good value close by to be compared to.

Additionally, they face another issue. Since the majority of our houses are being pumped out fast and repetitively, they can be built cheaply. The entire residential building industry is geared toward that mindset. From distribution and availability of materials to the skill level of labor, this particular assembly line is fine-tuned to spitting out these lifeless houses fast and cheaply by the millions. If you work on a one-off, everyone is asked to slow down and scratch their head. And with it, the cost of construction rises. For every head scratch, you are on the hook for another dollar.

A good framing crew of four or five, for instance, can pump out an average house within a few days. With all the studs, wood panel sheathing on the exterior, a few rolls of tar paper, and housing wrap, they create a thing that will look close to the final product. There are no surprises and no questions to be asked. And if something should not quite line up, they just find the solution on the fly. One working week and the entire house is framed. Just imagine throwing a monkey wrench into that. One innocent consideration of, let's say, a special porch roof for the entry with a handful of crafted details can nearly double the time this crew will need to work on a house. The framing of an entire house costs as much in labor and takes as long as a small special detail.

Since our houses are built on the cheap and the older neighborhoods might offer questionable comps, builders are confronted with some stark realities when they consider an infill lot. The cost of land plus the increased cost of construction will make the house more expensive than its neighbors.

And so the solution becomes to inject empty calories—that is, a multitude of empty square feet with the number of amenities and expensive rooms such as bathrooms and kitchens staying the same. It is a process that provides us with the bonus room and large open living spaces or oversized bedrooms, closets, and storage spaces. In defense of these builders, our ingrained nonsensical and industrial housing practices force them to build McMansions.

As for the ZIP Codes, we should add here briefly that they are valued either completely arbitrarily or intentionally to focus wealth into the pockets of a few. Throughout the past century, our financial institutions have developed redlined maps with districts deemed unsuitable for issuing loans to, from neighborhoods inhabited by newly minted Italian-American citizens to those of African-American descent and many in between. This practice, though no longer legal, had lasting consequences. Besides inequality in wealth and opportunities built by the few on the backs of many, it influenced enduring higher evaluations of some ZIP Codes over others. And where our power-hungry, greedy past does not suffice, we try it with fads and hype. We know of the neighborhoods that are trendy and desired, simply because we tell ourselves they are.

Average house prices shot up nearly 52 percent from 2015 through 2019 in McLennan County, Texas, home to Waco and the popular HGTV show *Fixer Upper* with Chip and Joanna Gaines,[11] simply for our need to keep up with the Joneses.

For You

_____

What does that leave for you, as you might consider creating a living environment that is meant for you to inhabit? Might I suggest for you to be aware of the myths and market forces we have looked at so far—that are there to respond to the many—and for you to ask for the specific instead? Try out these five simple considerations for size:

- Start with a Clean Slate

- Ignore the Real Estate Metrics

- Ask Yourself What You Are Looking For

- Understand You Are Asking for Art

- Love the Process

Start with a Clean Slate

Forget everything you have ever experienced a house might offer and start with a clean slate. Clearly, in most likelihood, the last one you lived in was cooked up on the back of a napkin in a boardroom by a developer who thought they built for far too much and charged you oh too little!

We certainly cannot complain about a lack of access to information. So go out there and look.

Look the world over for sexy and innovative residential architecture. You don't even have to leave the couch to scour the offerings of high-design magazines and online architectural platforms. And don't be too literal when you start out. It's not about the number of bedrooms or baths, or the number of stories. It's not even about the cost. It's all about what provides the goose bumps you deserve. Just start dreaming and stop being bogged down by prescriptive answers from the wrong people for the wrong reasons.

Ignore the Real Estate Metrics

If you create a house outside the nonsensical setup of appraisers, banks, and developers, you will create a home that will have to be sold on its true merits. The value then will not lie in the number of useless square feet, but in the structure's quality and spaces created. A unique one-of-a-kind home will sell for a unique one-of-a-kind price. Don't pump your hard-earned money into parameters that, when it comes to it, are not valued by anyone. Instead, pay for values that change your life in particular. Does that mean you will pay more? It does not. It will mean, however, you will pay more per square foot. But we already discovered that most of the square footage you have considered in the past, nobody uses or needs in the first place. And we have also found that the same amount of square footage can feel tight and claustrophobic or open and seemingly never ending, entirely dependent on the qualities with which the space you live in is created.

Ask Yourself What You Are Looking For

Allow yourself to listen to your desires and ask yourself what you are actually looking for. For instance, say to yourself that you would love to be awakened by the warm morning sun along a wide-open view of a tranquil natural setting. Maybe you would love to have a workstation, hardly larger than a desk that can lay bare your computer and stack of paperwork, yet vanish by a flick of your hand, forgotten as long as needed. Perhaps you would love to enjoy delicious meals as a family but prepare food in privacy. Maybe you would love to host boisterous festivities reminiscent of Hollywood's Golden Age or fully hide from the world instead. Maybe you would love to be burrowed into the earthen depths of a hill or flying high on stilts, cantilevering precariously over a treacherous cliff's edge. Or perhaps you paint, write, play music, repair cars, work out, tend to plants, build miniature railroad landscapes, or read. Ask for what might slumber deeply in your childhood dreams long forgotten. Be specific about the vague, about sensations of space, light, textures, and colors. Probe, ask, and wonder, for if this home is to be the stage for your life, a stage that will perpetuate the wonders of your own and only being, you need to start from the beginning with that which you crave.

Allow for the possibility of discovering something new. Either you have designed and built a custom home before—or at least you think you have—or your brother, best friend, or aunt has in the past. Or maybe you have seen a TV show and developed a sense of what the fuss is all about. I urge you to strip yourself of that sensation. Instead of building a house, what you really are asking for is the creation of a piece of livable art.

Understand You Are Asking for Art

With art, we search and grope through the unimaginable of ourselves—our existence. With art we guess, we wonder, we ask. With art we criticize. We briefly juxtapose synapses that ever so fleetingly make sense of it all. Actively creating art or passively consuming it—through it, our senses read senseless ideas and emotions. Art doesn't explain. It provides sense only for a moment. Art tugs at us. It forces us to engage because we have to. It is a ravenous and ambiguous beast.

Architecture at its best is all of that. And that is what you should ask to envelop yourself with. You should ask to wake up with excitement and wonderment on a daily basis for years to come. Picking cabinets or counters to falsely suggest you are somehow building a custom home is the furthest from it. Instead, ask for art!

Understand that you are not asking to walk down the aisle to pick a house off the shelf, or as it is, down the street of a new development. Those offerings are not created to provide a home for you. They are created for the masses, to be mass produced and cheaply made. Those houses are generic and created to the lowest common denominator. The very fact that you can buy those homes ready to go— sign here and move in—is a testimony to their meaninglessness. Instead, you are asking to create a home from scratch. And since you are, love the process!

Love the Process

You will find yourself engaged in an adventure of a lifetime. From selecting a property, to discovering and growing your dreams through the design process, to seeing it all materialize piece by piece, you will go through an emotional roller-coaster ride—a good one.

You will discover all new appreciations and understandings about you and your world. An entirely new set of sensations will surprise you. You will discover and be affected by a multitude of new spatial expressions, of unseen material textures and colors, of surprising musical variations on light and shadow, and of exhilarating stage sets expressed by forms, volumes, and structure.

You will also get to know and be intimately involved with a set of highly skilled professionals, trades, and artists who can't wait to enrich your life with the beauty they bring. When you ask for this, they will all come out of their burrows, face daylight, and take you on a ride of discovery, growth, and lasting happiness, and buoyancy. The more you open up for it, the more you will receive. The more you allow yourself to enjoy the ride, the richer the outcome will be.

Try it when you set out to create your own home. Follow these few simple steps and find out the best is yet to come.

》 Art doesn't explain. It provides sense only for a moment. Art tugs at us. It forces us to engage because we have to. It is a ravenous and ambiguous beast. From selecting a property, to discovering and growing your dreams through the design process, to seeing it all materialize piece by piece, you will go through an emotional roller-coaster ride—a good one. 《

Good Design Is Empathetic

You know you are experiencing good design when it seems like it knows you personally, when it reaches out to you and invites you in, when it understands your needs and listens to your worries.

We tried to achieve just that with a home, the Schönberg Residence, for a family of five. When we first set out, we did not have an inkling of the positive effect the home would ultimately have.

Three sisters, just a few years apart, received a wing of the home to themselves. They each were provided their own room, which we tried to shape properly with appropriate sizing, large floor-to-ceiling windows, and a potpourri of colors, each handpicked by the girls. We allowed these rooms to be an oasis of quietude and privacy for their individual sleep, play, and study.

Experiencing the great bond the sisters had and the family as a whole, it became apparent something else was needed. We looked for a binder, if you will, for the glue that was holding the family together. They have had the privilege of living in various spots around the world. Without a doubt, the continuous change in pace and culture allowed them to build a deep reliance on each other.

We created a climbing library for them. This was a space around which the three rooms of the sisters were grouped. It was barely five feet wide and climbed about three quarters of a story over a set of shelves and platforms. From the exterior, we treated it as an elongated red form that stuck out at either end of the building with cantilevering boxes. Along the way, the space changed in size and quality. On one end, there was a fortlike small cozy nook, just large enough to hold two to three kids (see Fig. 1, page 15). It had a large window overlooking the backyard playground. Around some of the seating platforms, complete with custom-made red cushions, the space was allowed to grow taller for a more open sense of freedom. The ceiling varied in height as it, too, climbed with the platforms below.

As a whole, bookshelves, cubbies, nooks, and crannies surrounded the entire space. Wood boxes were stacked on top of each other, set into the walls, holding books, toys, and the children. They got to sit, lean, sprawl, lay, and climb surrounded by the stuff made for pastime.

We kept the colors muted but warm in order to allow the mess of the children's play and daydreaming to be elevated to displayed art.

The narrowness of it all, and the various textures and sound-breaking niches, created quiet spatial eddies.

To our delight, all of this worked to the benefit of the family as hoped for. For instance, after moving in, the family shared with us that cleaning up for visitors was a nonexistent chore. Everything seemed to migrate into the myriad of boxes, shelves, and display cases by default. The stuff that was left around got pushed into the appropriate crevasses for the next moment of play to happen. Clutter seemed to vanish, simply because the inhabitable space was finite. And that which didn't vanish looked almost intentionally placed.

The clients had been open to some wild suggestions, such as dark, almost black, ceilings. Introducing a number of grays into a child's area of play must have been counterintuitive. But as a result, messes became the vestiges of a colorful life, beckoning for more playing, reading, and dreaming. They affirmed that the richness of curious probing, boredom, and adventurous travels of the creative mind are all supposed to happen and that those are, in fact, the child's sole job to fulfill.

After moving in, the family also discovered they could, all five of them, get comfortable, draped over the various steps and seats, and project a movie onto one of the adjacent walls. They created a built-in movie theater for a shared family experience. The terracing offered perfect individual seats, with handy trays for popcorn and drinks, grouping the audience together and joining them as a family.

The best story, though, was shared by the mother. She confided in us that she would find herself curled up in her blanket during sleepless nights on the topmost and largest cushioned area. Egged on by a mom's anxiety that knows no easing, she found this spot to be a cure for rest. She would lie snugly in between the rooms of her three blissfully sleeping daughters. That top spot of the climbing library stuck out among the surrounding treetops. The trees filtered moonlight into softly layered patterns of silvery light washing through tall windows on three sides of the top cantilever, where the sound was muffled to the point of creating a cocoon. Without knowing, we had created the very proverbial womb needed for the girls' mother to experience the calm and peace she desperately sought. It was a space that by its qualities in shape, materials, colors, sound, views, and flow turned into the perfect moment of serenity and deeply felt peace.

Fig. 9: The climbing library of the Schönberg Residence, 2010, Toby Witte.

Building blocks of **bliss**

Four pillars on which
to build your home.

Structure

To illustrate how the kind of spaces that have the potential to provide a place of happiness can be created, let me share with you four basic parts and qualities available to a design process. These, when considered well, are means by which to create a sense of home. Let's start with the structure.

The structure of your home is the stuff that holds up everything else. Like the skeleton in your body, it binds all the disparate pieces of a built environment together. It carries heavy loads and conducts weight to the ground, allowing gravity to assert its hold.

The structure is exposed to many forces. A simple beam wants to twist and bend, twirl and break.

Structure depends on its materiality. While thin steel might prefer to act like tendons in your leg, brute concrete would appreciate a pounding. A vertical wooden post might oblige to quite a bit of weight if it's directed along its grain—against the grain and it might splinter. Against the grain, however, a horizontal wood beam might gently bend, or, at the right pressure point, shear off with ease.

Structure is also dependent on its application. While a sheet of paper would be hard-pressed to hold itself up, let alone an entire roof, thickly spun paper tubes can span and carry vast expanses of space and coverings, respectively.

Beyond the physics of it all, a stylized structure can deconstruct the elements that define the space you create, offering a pristine confidence to your home besides just elegance and style.

Structure exposed has the power to bear your understanding of yourself within the world you inhabit.

Often, structural elements are hidden within complex assemblies. If you take apart a wall, for example, you will find that it is tasked to resolve many technical issues besides those considered by a structural engineer. The wall that boxes in your living room, let's say, a mere six inches thick, is finished with a painted surface on the interior and some ubiquitous siding material on the outside. Yet it is asked to hold up a floor and a roof. It has to withstand raging winds; keep the interior temperature markedly different from the exterior; separate different moisture content of the air on either side; repel rain, hail, and snow;

provide air movement to dry out each of its layers, preventing mold and rot; house utility runs such as ducts, pipes, and cables; offer openings for views, fresh air, and egress; and deliver the potential for a visceral reaction by way of its color, texture, and materiality.

It is not surprising that this wall is created out of many different pieces. But if you allow yourself to take a look, regard each component, and start to play and elevate a few or all of its tasks, there will be a chance for beauty to ensue—beauty in the object that is your home and beauty in how you experience yourself within it.

When we removed the structural portion of the walls in the Gerendák Residence, we found ourselves moving down that particular rabbit hole—discovering a magic we did not seek at first.

As for the structure and its primary purpose of holding things up, we conceived of a set of wood beams and posts—all visible to the naked eye. Spaced five feet apart, we erected identical assemblies of architectural glulam beams. These are considered to be "engineered lumber," created by gluing small wood pieces together, offering not only tremendous structural abilities but also a suave, stratified look. Each assembly comprised two pairs of eighteen-inch-tall, horizontal beams that sandwiched a single, vertical post of the same size on either end. There was a horizontal pair to stand on and another to carry a roof. The vertical post connected each of the two horizontal bands and suspended the upper set.

Both the floor and the roof were visually created as two flat slabs resting on those horizontal pairs of beams. At first, we sized the wood elements to meet structural concerns. In part, they simply had to hold weight, but also combat shear and deflection, as we let these assemblies cantilever into thin air on one end. However, we adjusted the sizing and spacing purely to balance their proportions. We asked for each assembly to look right by itself and to each other. They also had to find the right physical presence to define properly the space between each group of horizontal sets and the views left in between.

Since the vertical posts were only three and a half inches thick but eighteen inches deep, they almost vanished from sight when looking past them toward the major lake views. When looking at them from

Fig. 10: Main living space of the Gerendák Residence, 2022, Toby Witte.

the side, however, they appeared visually beefed up, strongly encapsulating the space they surrounded.

We also made use of a simple but effective classicist trick to work the proportions of the overall setup. Just as the Greek master builders of temples two and a half millennia ago, we narrowed the outer two bays to four and a half feet—offering a stouter compactness along the edges of the home.

With the structure removed from the walls, we had nothing left but open space all around the posts. We filled it with nothing but glass, providing views, double-glazed insulation, and rain and moisture protection all in one.

The walls of glass did not hold up anything but themselves. We were left to place them anywhere within this structural setup. And so we created an open-air terrace next to an enclosed living area, moving the glass within the wood structure to separate the two.

The benefits were many. For one, the sets of beams sliding along the underside of the flat roof continued past this glass separation, effectively softening the delineation between the interior and exterior. One wasn't quite certain where the inside stopped and the outside began. In turn, this also caused the living room to feel about twice as large as it actually was.

This structural setup also allowed us to insert a light shelf, a slightly lower roof over the terrace. This dropped plane defined the smaller space of the terrace appropriately for cozy lounging and contracted the expansive views across the open lake, which was necessary to keep your senses grounded and gaze focused. This secondary roof also reflected natural light onto the living room ceiling and acted as a visor against solar gain, benefiting a natural light management described below (see page 100).

In addition, we used the set of vertical posts as stationary shutters, blocking the low evening sun entering from the lake—a problem usually met with blinds that manage to negate all good views as well. The sunset is about the worst light to combat with mechanical means. It effectively bakes your home. Here, however, the views were left open and simultaneously shielded from the sun at its worst angle.

Despite all the practical and functional benefits of this structural setup, the ultimate advantage of it, and its true motivation for being, was the poetic connection to the natural landscape it provided. The growth of vertical wood posts both stylized and visually continued the thicket of tall tree trunks surrounding the home. They also filtered the view to the expanse of water and further blurred the lines, which paid homage to the natural world.

As for the homeowners, more importantly, and their sense of self, it should be said that singling out the building elements defining the primary space of this home and highlighting the structure had a profound effect. The moves described, the extraction of simple forms and structural members, showcasing their functions and effects, seemed to simplify the entire arrangement, all the while introducing a gentle complexity. The roof, a simple slab, held off rain. The beams, sized and paired to be recognized, held up the roof. The posts, slender and many, held up the beams. The glass, vast and void of structure, provided views and retained heat, keeping the occupants warm. The singularity of each piece, in turn, aggrandized the presence of the homeowners themselves within the space. It allowed them to feel as just another part of the ensemble. The elements of the home, those of the surrounding nature, and the inhabitants themselves—all played along as simple and distinct parts of a whole.

And conversely, with all the elements finding a distinct presence, the boundaries between inside and out, the man-made and nature, the structure and well-being, and the person and the ephemeral, were blurred.

And as the parts of the building revealed themselves distinctly, as they were prevented from hiding, so were the occupants rendered in sharper relief. The honesty in structure allowed for honesty in being.

Space

Space, in the world of architecture, is defined as an inhabitable volume.

We all know well the feeling of such an incorporeal presence. As children, we build a space out of blankets. As adults, we pull chairs around a campfire and get lost in a few hours of comradery. With space there is a place, a function, a geometry. And with space, there is a quality of home.

The metaphorical womb is a space imbued with the qualities of warmth and protection. The space of a cathedral has the quality of hollowed grandeur reaching to the heavens, offering a distinctly different experience than that of a subway station. A mountaintop has a unique sense of place compared to that of a forest. Each instance engages us differently and plucks our strings in particular ways.

This sense of space is a fundamental part of our understanding of ourselves within the world. Good design plays on that. Good design finds just the right elements to create a sense of space.

Good design finds the right textile qualities—whether cold, warm, rough, liquid, smooth, or airy. It finds the right play of light and shadow—brightly washed out, rippled by beams of light, or cast in darkness. Thoughtful design asks for help from such elements as impenetrable cells, open walls, floating planes, singular posts, far-reaching beams, or just a nearly indistinct marker on the ground. They all play with our senses to stir up emotions, toy with desires, generate thoughts, and awaken memories. Space can be big or small, cold or cozy, invigorating or calm, menacing or inspiring, happy or solemn.

Space offers a sense of place, an idea of home, tying into the perceived and real history of its inhabitants, their commonality and shared story.

Famed architect Zaha Hadid once said that "architecture is how the person places herself in the space. Fashion is about how you place the object on the person."[12] As the quality of space has an essential effect on our sense of ourselves, it is on architecture to work it carefully. The careful consideration and creation of that space is maybe the most important task of architecture. In it lies its art.

Picasso is known to have said he never did "a painting as a work of art. All of them are researches," and "when it is finished, [a picture] still goes on changing, according to the state of mind of whoever is looking at it. A picture lives a life like a living creature, undergoing the changes imposed on us by our life from day to day."[13] For architecture, the canvas is space.

Effectively, space is the incorporeal form defined by the very elements we throw about and think of as our home. Our home, however, really is the pregnant void in between. The consideration of space is the most pressing concern in the creation of our homes. In the end, after all the work necessary to erect and arrange things, the purpose of the whole undertaking is to create a space—one worth living in.

Space is a fluid form that has an inherent need to spread and flow. Think of it like a body of water running through a riverbed, as it gently nudges around rocks and through crevasses, and is pooling in spots.

Space wants to move on. When we hold it in place for a moment, we create a palpable tension. The entry of the Pantheon famously tightens as you

Fig. 11: Pantheon, Rome, 126 AD.

enter from the passages and small piazzas of the Eternal City, only to release you into a vast, open, round-domed space that ultimately culminates in a small oculus at its apex. A bird would fly right through. The space does too. The contraction-release-contraction-release of that movement intensifies the awe of the experience. It offers repose and yet itches one to move on and wonder about the unknowable beyond—the pantheon of gods.

When done right, the space itself turns into pure form. You can almost touch it. When done right, all the elements defining it will dissipate from your awareness.

Chances are you have visited the Vietnam Veterans Memorial in Washington, DC. Designed by Maya Lin in 1981, it remains arguably the most personally affecting space in all of North America.

It has weakened my knees at every visit. I do not claim to have any personal relationship to the Vietnam War or know of family members who have died in its pursuit (and I apologize to anyone who has a deeper relationship to this memorial and to whom a mere architectural appreciation is not enough). Even so, when I have walked up to the tip of one of its ends and descended into the ground, sliced into by two stark sheets of polished black granite, I have been profoundly overwhelmed by a sadness literally grounded in the deep folds of the earth.

A few simple stylized forms shape this memorial—a space with tremendously tactile qualities. As I moved past the wall, the ground swallowed me on one side, while on the other

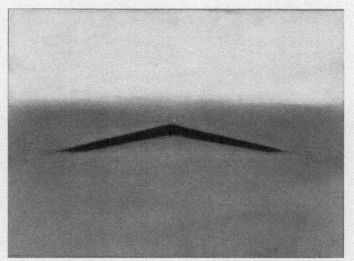

Fig. 12: Competition Entry to the Vietnam Memorial competition, 1981, Maya Lin.

it sloped safely up, releasing me to the open air. The further I went in, the more complete and enveloping the space became. Yet all it took was two walls, black and smooth, carving a gentle dip into the ground. It is incredibly simple and incredibly effective.

When you create your own home, it will be of utmost importance to understand the type of space you are asking for and the qualities it needs. And remember, most often, just like with the Vietnam Veterans Memorial, you are not asking for four walls and a roof. The chest of tools allows for more.

» As children, we build a space out of blankets. As adults, we pull chairs around a campfire and get lost in a few hours of comradery. With space there is a place, a function, a geometry. And with space, there is a quality of home. «

Texture
_____

Brick, I stipulate, belongs inside the house. We already consider brick to be a luxury. After all, some of us prefer to live in a house faced with it, often displaying it to the street and relying on cheaper siding for the remaining elevations. We tend to place it where we can show to the world we can afford it.

However, its real luxury does not lie in its sticker price, but rather in its materiality. Brick is heavy and somehow conveys its weight from a distance. It seems cold, earthen, and grounded. It appears as if gravity begs the brick to return to the very earth it originated from. Born out of mud and minerals, it is nothing less than a part of the primeval sludge from which all living things are created and eventually restored to.

Masonry walls and their parts come in many shapes and forms. The basic brick units can be long, tall, thin, or thick—or any proportion you can think of. There are different colors and textures to choose from. Whether gray and rough, or black and oily, or terra cotta and dull, as kaleidoscopic as desert sands are the options for the brick's substance.

To create a wall, we can choose the mortar, the binding glue, to be slim or wide, dark or light, coarse or smooth, troweled or pointed. The wall itself can be straight or curved, heavy or thinly applied. It can be structural or lifted onto toothpicks or even deconstructed.

What the masonry wall provides to our living environment from a sensual perspective is a texture rich in variation. It returns nature to the fabricated structure. It creates surfaces that are refracting light and sound in ever-changing patterns. A liveliness that belies the brick's seemingly dormant state. It provides strength, protection, warmth, and safety. If you were to place a masonry wall as a freestanding form into the untouched landscape, I bet we would all migrate to it, lean against it, and then set up camp adjacent to it.

When my family and I designed and built our own home, we drew from this very quality. We placed an eight-foot-tall and forty-foot-long straight masonry wall made of grayish-brown, dusty, standard-sized brick and black, recessed mortar onto a clearing and laid out the living spaces all around it.

The wall, a good foot and a half thick, cut through the entire house, projecting out several feet at the front. The main entry and interior stairs, the two most important points of circulation, hugged the wall and forced one up close several times during the day. You found yourself near enough to touch it and to run your fingers over the rough surface.

The downstairs was essentially a loft-like living arrangement with all the primary spaces for cooking, eating, lounging, and sleeping for the parents while the children resided above. Those downstairs spaces pinwheeled around the brick wall, decreasing in scale and increasing in privacy as you moved around it. They commenced from the area that held the large kitchen and dining table, the communal center of our home, and moved to the cozier area of couches and chairs where we read in private or watched television as a family. Then they continued to move to the main bedroom area that opened up to the living room by a set of room-high sliding panels. At the end, a bathroom, asking for the most intimacy, precluded the procession and hugged the wall tightly on its long side for the most protection.

Fig. 13: The main living area of the Witte Home, 2017, Toby Witte.

The sliding panels were open during the day and allowed our sleeping quarters to lend their square feet to the rest of the house and sequester them for full privacy during the night.

In the process of piercing itself through our daily routines, like the skewer of a shish kebab, the brick wall weaved through other elements of the home, such as the stairs, pantry and laundry, built-in shoe storage at the entry, and closet niches. The brick wall was omnipresent, not in its entirety, but partially in the background as it vanished and reappeared. It provided a strong backbone to our daily life and suggested stability, safety, and calmness. It also lent a sense of self-assurance to the surrounding spaces. They acted as if they were meant to be where they were. As if they had always been there. They were not going anywhere. Not even a tornado would have taken them away, whether the roof remained or was gone for good.

It is important to mention that the brick did not appear to have been applied in this example. The wall sat there, discernible in its entirety. Exiting a car or walking up from a stroll, we engaged with one end, the exterior portion, freestanding, thick and heavy. We saw it and perceived it as an actual wall. The other end stuck into the bedroom area, eight feet tall under a nine-foot ceiling. There, too, it was freestanding. It flaunted its dimensions. There was a height to the wall, a width, and a length. Your body instinctively measured and remained aware of it. There was a corporeal recognition. You knew its presence. It was there like

Fig. 14: The main bedroom area of the Witte Home, 2017, Toby Witte.

a good friend, dependable, reliable, unwavering, and unconditional.

That wall, the brick, the earthen texture provided a richness and luxuriousness to nearly every moment of our domestic life because it was part of our inhabitable spaces. This brick was mostly in the interior of our home, where it belonged and was given the opportunity to lend all of its properties to our self-awareness. There, it had a chance to provide a positive influence on how we experienced each moment of the day and ourselves in it.

In a similar manner, all the materials with which we define the spaces we live in generally have specific textural qualities. And in similar ways, we can recognize and harness those qualities. We can play with them deliberately, much like we play the keys on a piano to craft endless variations of melodies that we can recognize and react to. And just like a few notes have the power to change our emotions in an instance, so do the textures of the materials we build with.

When we draw from the near infinite array of possibilities in materials and textures, we have a chance to address the specifics of the environment we crave.

>> In a similar manner, all the materials with which we define the spaces we live in generally have specific textural qualities. And in similar ways, we can recognize and harness those qualities. We can play with them deliberately. <<

Light and Shadows

Another engaging aspect of that wall and its texture in my family's home was the constantly changing play of light and shadow washing over it.

A building comes to life when the sun interacts with its surfaces, whether directly or filtered through layers of permeable materials. Light can be considered as one of the most important, yet most ephemeral, building materials. When we think of our home literally as a stage set for our daily life, the interaction of light and shadow are the lighting design for the performance.

A space can drastically change its mood depending on the quality of the natural light. A brightly lit morning breakfast nook might be invigorating and welcoming, setting the tone for you on how to tackle the upcoming day's tasks. A softly lit window seat might ask you to climb in, curl up, and read a book. Or a warm evening sun cascading gently along a rough vertical concrete surface might relax you just enough to pour a glass of your favorite drink and allow you to forget about any pressing concerns.

In the example of the Schönberg Residence for the family of five (see page 68), I described how the moonlight, filtered by adjacent trees, left gently moving patterns on the surfaces surrounding the platform that allowed the mother to find a peaceful sleep. It created a gentle ripple of silvery light, small blotches with soft overlapping edges, forming a constantly shifting and rearranging mosaic. It was yet another moment where music was stylized into a built reality without a sound made and eliciting a profound emotional and sensual reaction.

Part of the power behind this arrangement, here too, was the connection to something greater than the family's immediate surroundings. The light of the star at the center of our solar system was reflected off the surface of another planetary body. It refracted through layers of an omnipresent nature, which we ourselves might think to be just another minute part of, creating a most gentle blanket to be enveloped with. It allowed the homeowners to know that the space they found themselves in not only extended to the exterior, beyond the built walls, but much farther. The expansive sense of this very setting had the potential to calm them down and provide them with a notion of deeply felt peace.

To allow for this opportunity of natural light to be distinctly expressed is then our responsibility to create.

When we worked on the design of the Schönberg Residence, we were confronted with a south-facing expanse of glass. We introduced an open windowed side to expose the common areas of the girls' wing to the backyard. Through it, the sisters were able to see each other, no matter where the playing took place. It also projected the lush natural setting into the interior, enlarged the space without adding square feet, and filled the home with a bright friendly light.

The southern light happens to be the best to manage from a solar gain perspective. The consideration here is to allow the rays of the low winter sun inside to warm up a home and, conversely, to keep them out during the summer, when the sun sits high in the sky, to reduce any cooling efforts. One easy way to do this is with awnings placed above windows or glass facades. Picture the visor on a baseball cap shading your eyes and allowing for views.

Fig. 15: Awning at the Schönberg Residence, 2010, Toby Witte.

In the case of the Schönberg Residence, we calculated a four-and-a-half-foot wide shield to do the trick. We inserted steel posts in between each three-foot-wide and seven-foot-tall fixed glass window and welded horizontal arms to their top. Those, in turn, held a set of flat aluminum panels to create the visor. Above each tall window and the awning, we added a narrow hopper window that could be opened to the interior for a breeze. Light was reflected off the shiny flat metal through the narrow slit of the top row of hoppers and livened up the ceiling. In the meantime, the awning did its work for the tall portion of the glass facade, keeping out or letting in natural light with slowly changing intensity throughout the seasons.

So far, so good. However, we wondered how we could go a step further in managing the natural light. In addition, we needed to resolve the weight of rainwater puddling on the aluminum panels. We wanted to keep them as thin as possible with no additional visually bulky support structure.

We opted for a perforation, a pattern of holes with specific sizing and density. After trial and error, it provided just enough playful lighting through the panels and enough shading on the windows to alleviate our energy concerns. Our goal was to see a playful polka dot pattern of moving light engaging the dark wood floor and adjacent walls—changing its position steadily during the course of a day. The shape and sharpness of the pattern would adjust with the sun's intensity throughout the year.

What we again did not account for and wish we could say we planned, was that the moon wanted to play just the same—these changes happening on a faster, monthly cycle. As a result, a pattern of moonlight gently sprinkled the very path the mother took on the aforementioned sleepless nights. Just imagine sneaking softly through this field of quiet lighting along the children's fragile sleeping quarters, as if you were wading through soft reflections of whirls and pools of distant cosmic rivers that offer a nod to the world as it takes its planetary turns. Imagine experiencing this moment, only to climb the library and find a deep respite in an even gentler and more naturally arrived version of the same on that quiet, peaceful top landing.

This treatment of light and shadow turned out to be a formal and spatial expression that affected a poetic approach to the housing of a family. It was sparse in materiality and yet powerful in its assertion.

Before you flip the page and as you consider the creation of your own home, please remember the four aspects of a built environment we looked at here. When considered correctly, they will have a chance to turn your home into inhabitable art:

- Structure

- Space

- Texture

- Light and Shadows

Tugging at bliss

A closer look at a few of the realities that shape the creation of our homes, how they came to be, and how we might treat them.

Architects

It might seem easy enough to move forward with these building blocks that promise a better way of life. All we would have to do is to ask ourselves what it is we are asking for in our homes, understand the riches available to us, and, with a creative spirit, find answers in the built form. However, as we have glimpsed at previously we are burdened with preconceived notions, self-inflicted harm, and cultural and market forces we blindly subscribe to.

Let's take a closer look at a few of these systems and straitjackets at play that shape our decision-making in creating our homes. I hope to help you form a picture of the status quo and how one could endeavor to engage with it for a better outcome. To start with, let's look at who is behind the creative spark.

The profession of architecture has a long history and has undergone many changes. Arguably, since the Renaissance, or at least a handful of centuries ago, the designers behind some of the works of art shaping our built environment have become names to be recognized and sought after.

What we find these days in the United States is an entirely different field of practice.

The image of the star architect still populates the public imagination and a few of them make their rounds on social media and a few documentaries— the genius lone lead designer who, with a stroke of the pen, drops a napkin sketch and creates built forms. In fact, iconic buildings are still considered to be "built" by the architect. Of course, architects don't build. They design and they advise. The creation of a building covers a large range of services, of which the singular designer fills only a very narrow slice.

There are roughly sixty-five thousand architecture firms in the US these days, populated by about one hundred twenty thousand licensed and many more unlicensed architects. Only roughly 7.5 percent of their revenue is earned through the work on single-family houses.[14]

The path to accreditation for a licensed architect takes about twelve years. In general, they enter as an idealist at best, or an unimaginative teenager pushed by a guidance counselor at worst, and exit as technocrats. It is not unusual to see their professional development begin as art and end in the pushing of code books, zoning restrictions, and ever-reducing outlays of margin-driven developers. For the most part, architects are undervalued facilitators of the mundane. They are asked to provide the bare minimum instructions on how to build a building in order for investors to draw a profit. Creativity in those cases is not only shunned—it is to be avoided. Time is money. Money is what most buildings get built for. In the United States, architects have become a necessary evil, for the most part.

Luckily, however, architectural offices are varied in their size and offerings. Who then are those brilliant minds I have mentioned before that can lead the charge for the successful creation of a home designed just for you?

Your heroes hide in small firms from one to a dozen professionals. They make up about three-quarters of all firms, but cover far less than a quarter of all employees and workload.[15] Among those firms, you will find the ones who will provide the kind of singular attention and creativity you seek. While most architects work in bigger firms on bigger projects, you should look for the smaller firms that offer the mindset necessary to create miracles.

You will also find them among many of those entities that are run by unlicensed residential designers.

A brief excurse into the discussion of licensure might be necessary here. In each state of the US, an architectural licensing board doles out licenses to architects after rigorous testing. However, in most jurisdictions, the long tentacles of their laws and statutes do not reach the creation of single-family homes. Their necessity is well placed in the commercial world, where the public realm asks for public supervision, the insurance of common standards. That is when we talk about the kind of mixed-use urban projects we mentioned in the beginning of the book (see page 20). However, as discussed, a single-family home is there for your joy only. Here you are asking for a particular design genius, the bedrock of which is dedication, intent, and purposefulness. Luckily, that expands your search to unlicensed residential design firms and design-build companies as well.

In fact, whether licensed architecture offices, residential design professionals, or design-build outfits, you will be most successful with those firms whose focus lies entirely on single-family homes. Those are the experts you seek.

In addition, nearly all projects—even the single-family home—will require a team of designers. It is rare that for any substantial building, including your home, a single person will be enough to cover all the tasks at hand. In bigger firms, on larger projects, a design director—not a star architect—will develop an idea and pass it on to a hive of worker bees. They will certainly be proficient in their technical abilities. However, in the right small firm you will find a dedicated team, one that not only has developed its understanding of practical concerns, but also has thrived on its ability to be creative and to approach your home with intent.

Of all architecture firms, only about half are concentrated on a single narrow field, in which they are experts. The other half make up general practitioners, the proverbial master of all and expert in none, or consultants and related fields.[16]

Your task will be to find a small firm that is specialized in your type of home and one that has not lost their love for and ability to create art. Avoid all others.

As a matter of fact, you are asking for your entire team to be just that—all your designers, engineers, the general contractor, and building crews. You are looking for those few brilliant souls who love their craft, are experts in their field, and can guide you through the entire process. From finding a property, designing your dream, building it into reality, all the way to moving in.

I hope I have made it clear by now that you are not going to ask for a set of "blueprints." The drawings, the paperwork, are going to be a mere by-product of the actual work, which is the creative act. You are asking for more than a few lines on paper. You are asking to be heard and understood. You are asking for an exploration into your true motivation and desires. And you are asking to be safely guided through the process.

The creative process should be a discovery into the unknown, revealing the most innovative, empathetic, and artful outcome possible. Your home should ultimately be a reflection of you. Your home should be a distillation of how you live. And just as you are unique in who you are, so will be the home you are asking for.

Fig. 16: Creative session and client meeting, Toby Witte.

Working with the right design team should be a joyful adventure. The right ones will come with the depth of knowledge necessary to create your home. They will address the ideas ensconced in this book and then some. They will, of course, also address and safely maneuver the project around practical concerns, such as the building codes, site requirements, and your budget. They will also draw up a set of construction drawings for you, the IKEA assembly instructions, if you will.

However, those skills are baked in and are the minimum of service they should offer.

The true measure of value you will seek is in their creative muscle for the specific and their expertise to consult on the entirety of the project.

» Your home should ultimately be a reflection of you. Your home should be a distillation of how you live. And just as you are unique in who you are, so will be the home you are asking for. «

The Cost

_____

When you ask for a well-designed home, a place that is specific to your needs and desires, that is considered, looked at, and crafted, that is an art piece, that is empathetic and sympathetic, that validates your own luxury, that will knock your socks off, is innovative and fresh, that explores your own being, and that supports your own unique life's past, present, and future, you ask for something more. And when you ask for something more, you will have to pay for more.

We have already talked about how the real estate market is solely valuing square feet and a ZIP Code and how we have come to measure both through precedents provided by a mass production industry.

When you ask to create a true home for yourself, you operate on a different playing field, and you need to judge the dollar spent on different parameters.

Everyone has their budget, a specific amount they can spend. That amount should be honored. The question becomes what you want to spend it on. Here are several ways to consider it, several passes on how to look at it from different angles.

- This is a conversation I have had in some shape or form with almost every single client. Imagine you just stopped by for an initial consultation to understand what you are in for. Over a cup of coffee, we have addressed all of your big questions and concerns and are making it to the consideration of cost. And you will have said your mother, brother, best friend, or boss just built a mansion, eight thousand square feet in size and only so many dollars per square foot in price. You will ask why you should pay twice as much or three times as much or six times as much. And then imagine hearing me say this:

"I don't want you to pay more. I just want you to pay for what you are yearning for. You have come to me because you want a Maserati and you compare it to a school bus. By the metrics of the real estate market, the school bus provides more than the engineered machine of luxury, power, beauty, and driving pleasure. The school bus is bigger—much bigger even. It is available for a far better per-square-foot price. However, in hard-earned dollars, they cost the same. The sticker price is the same. But the Maserati is more expensive in your estimation. The per-square-foot price is ridiculously higher. You come to me because you want a Maserati, but you talk about paying for a school bus. You love, you crave, you lust for this masterpiece. It has an engine that purrs like a kitten when you rev it around hairpin mountain turns. It glides as smooth as a ballerina into lower gear. It cushions your tush on hand-stitched, custom-tanned hides, softened by forms that have been studied and studied again to mold themselves to your particular physique. It is engineered, considered, and crafted repeatedly, down to the last detail—so much so that only the best possible version of a driving apparatus is the outcome. And yet you think to say you don't understand why you should pay more per square foot than for that school bus.

"You are asking for luxury. So pay for luxury and feel good about it. There is no shame in it. You earned it. You pay the same amount, so why not pay for what you desire?

"Are you telling me the Maserati is too small for the two of you cruising to your vacation spot on the coast? Are you asking to trade in all of this goodness for a hundred more square feet of empty rattling tin and noisy constant screeching? You are not in the market for a school bus. A school bus will not bring you happiness. And yes, this analogy has plenty of holes, but everyone has their own Maserati, with its own price point that fits their own particular pocket book and sense of luxury. So go for it. Pay for what matters. Don't be obsessed with square feet. Square feet are not what will make you happy."

- Next, in that same conversation, you will say, "But what about the resale value?" You will have said this will be your forever home but rightfully wish you can pass it on to your children.

The short of it is, if you are willing to pay for it, so will the next owner. This home will not be a mass-produced commodity for the many, but one of those rare finds of which too few exist. You will be able to set your price, or your children will—a price that will be outside the common real estate metrics.

• From a different angle, consider this. Don't take the precedents of the mass-production industry as a starting point. The cost of construction for those houses is the outlier, since they were built on the assembly line. That cost is not a reflection of building homes. It reflects mass production. The actual cost of construction is an entirely different thing. When you are actually crafting a built environment with skilled craftspeople and materials selected specifically for you, with a loving eye and a caring hand, you are asking for what it actually costs to build a home.

In today's market, one hundred and fifty dollars per square foot is the crazy abnormality born out of mass production. A number twice that, or a multitude of it, will be closer to the actual cost of construction. But it doesn't really matter since we don't measure your success by square footage, but rather by quality of life.

• Another way to look at it is by valuing the art—to value your home as an art piece. Imagine walking into a gallery or auction house and considering buying a Picasso by the square footage.

I hope you will allow yourself instead to pay for the creative act, the depth of artistic expression that will enrich your life, and the status. Yes, it is an investment. I am sure you can get a knockoff print at the local craft store for a fraction of the cost. But who is asking?

- And lastly you will say: "I know. I know. I know. But still, why does it cost so much? What am I paying for?"

To answer that, let's consider three different simple staircases for easy comparison. The first is carpeted and tugged between two simple walls of sheetrock and paint. The second is finished with hardwood, sharp edges, no bullnoses, a brick wall on one side, openness on the other, niches carved into adjacent walls, and storage built into the steps. And the third is a custom-crafted floating staircase, with heavy weathered and handpicked wood treads on a slender steel structure and a cable steel railing—nothing but air, simplicity, craft, and beauty.

- The first staircase is about the most cost-effective way to build a staircase. The substructure could be of the cheapest materials and labor; it could even be pre-manufactured. The carpet will cover all sins. The sidewalls, too, require little skill. Any framing and drywall crew can pull this off. No one will have questions. Everyone knows what to do. It is mundane and thousands of these are being built at this very moment as you are reading these lines. It does not matter where the drywall is purchased from or what carpet will be chosen. Any color paint will be available. No thought goes into the design and construction of this one, and no thought will come out of it.

• The second staircase will take more labor and specialized skill. The treads and risers themselves will have to involve a fine woodworker. The substructure has to be precise and built to spec. The woodworker will have to acquire the right kind of wood that matches the surrounding flooring. It has to be dried, planed, cut, sanded, and finished. The no-bullnose simple edges require precision cutting and joining. Each tread and riser will have to be field measured and adjusted if necessary. And then it has to be installed, piece by piece in the field, gently hammered into place, glued, and touched up. There will be many questions

Fig. 17: The first staircase at the Lydia Avenue Home, 2019, Toby Witte.

and choices exchanged between designer, fine woodworker, general contractor, building trades, and homeowners. It all will take longer and you will definitely see some heads being scratched. The entire upgrade described, of course, was just for what we were replacing the carpet with.

- On the third staircase, every piece is designed down to the last screw and weld line. A structural engineer will have to be included. We now have, besides the custom woodworker, a specialized steel craftsperson. The thick wood slabs will ask for creativity, skill, and expertise. They shall keep their shape over the years. You will need the type of craftsperson who has done something like this a few times before. The cable railing itself becomes a piece of art. The section of the codebook about stairs is thick, and since this is a one-off-design, everyone has to be on their toes, double-checking, measuring twice, and cutting once. The materials are much more pristine and expensive, and the labor is too. The design will take longer, will be more in-depth, and collaborative. As for the head scratching, don't even bother to lower the hand. But the beauty of it all will be magnificent. If ever someone will glide down a staircase in style, it will be this one.

Fig. 18: The second staircase at the Witte Home, 2017,
Toby Witte.

We all seek a home. And we all deserve one. But when we try to find it in a single-family house, the standalone entity, we have to be honest and admit we just can't all afford one. A house is a luxury. A home meets an innate desire that is personal and specific. Sometimes you can be lucky enough to turn a mass-produced structure into some amalgam of home and straitjacket, a found object that you made work.

When you ask to create this home from scratch, your hard-earned money will go everywhere but square feet. It will be spent purely on quality. There is no choice. You are asking for it. Trust it and go for it. You will be rewarded every single day for years to come.

Fig. 19: The third staircase at the Gillingham Strauss Residence, 2017, Toby Witte.

The Size of Happiness

_____

The previous analogy of the Maserati and the school bus is one to dwell on for a moment. It goes to the heart of this book. Or rather, it allows you to dismantle one of the biggest hurdles you will face as you are considering the future of your home. It is likely you have been conditioned to think more square feet are better and a luxury in itself. And chances are you also instinctively surmise this might not be true.

At the beginning, smartphones were ostensibly sold as a replacement for the wall-hung crank of a phone, or at least their modern-day equivalent. Of course, they were in reality a personal computer that fit into your pocket. We have caught up by now and have switched our preferred way of communication to the shortest snippets of text and text abbreviations sent through the ether over a multitude of interchangeable platforms. And that slab in our pocket has powered up to a degree in computing prowess that far exceeds anything used half a century ago to send human beings to the surface of the moon. The smartphone is anything but a phone. You can still buy a phone that you can plug into a wall. The cost of it is a fraction of the former. However, you do not question the disparity in price.

That switch in the value proposition of the smartphone compared to the phone of a bygone era is in our rearview mirror. You do not question the exorbitant prices, despite the fact that your impressive machines of computing far exceed your needs. None of us will ever fully use all their services or technological potential.

If I were to tell you grandmother's wall-hung unit is far cheaper per square foot, you would shake your head incredulously. And so you should. What does it matter? A smartphone is more expensive per unit of size than the old home phone. Sure, it offers so much more. Why wouldn't it? Consider the same about the size of your home.

Of course, your home asks to be of a certain size. Any function needs a certain space to be elegantly executed in. Your sense of space and its need for a specific set of qualities translates into distinct proportions and spread. A design crafted for these considerations will reveal a certain size of home, one that square feet or volume could measure. However, there is no inherent value in whatever number that might be. In fact, that number could come out differently depending on how all your needs and requirements are met in built form. It is completely arbitrary and in no relation to how you value the quality of your home.

To approach your design team saying, "Give me more cubic feet, or square meters, or linear ells" is utterly void of meaning. On the other hand, to approach your design team asking for a built environment that allows you to be happier, more fulfilled, tickled by sensual riches, provided with more emotional depth, and enriched by a heightened sense of self is essential. That is how asking for a home should be verbalized. If we should stoop so low to measure anything with a yardstick, it should be the size of your smile.

Smartphones became smaller in volumetric size at one point, and then larger again as we turned off our TVs and relied on these pocket screens for entertainment. There is a size that works well to make a phone call. And there is a size that works well for watching a video clip or a full-fledged movie. We do not brag about either. We brag about other qualities we see in these devices. And we happily pay for those, whatever the cost, and then some.

Fig. 20: View of the living area and terrace toward the enclosed breezeway of the Gerendák Residence, 2022, Toby Witte.

To supersize your bliss, task your design team to cut out all wasteful, unused, and unappreciated square feet in order to increase the quality of your surroundings. What else is there to omit to make you happier? What else is there to cut to allow for an increased spaciousness? What else can we remove to supercharge your luxury? Give me less so I can have more.

The task here then is to decrease the size of your home so for the same budget you can receive more richness. Instead of adding a guest bedroom that only gets used two weeks in the year, consider powering up the spaces you use yourself.

The higher the square-foot price, the higher your happiness. The smaller the house, the more money is left for what's important to you. So ask to make it more expensive per square foot. Keep the budget you have and ask for the best home possible. Saturate your home with goodness.

》If we should stoop so low to measure anything with a yardstick, it should be the size of your smile. 《

Time

Another and arguably better metric by which to measure your home is time—or as an extension, cost per time. We spend an inordinate amount of time in our homes—since the onset of the last global pandemic, even more so.

For most of us mere mortals, time moves only in one direction—forward. The moments we spend in our home arrange themselves one after another. All impregnated by the quality of our surroundings. At its worst are the ice-cold windowless walls of a prison cell. At its best, it is the rich, light-filled environment you seek. Chances are your home is the one space that will influence your psyche most of your time. It will carry the most significance. After all, it is your sanctuary. The time spent here marches on. Until it doesn't. Time for us is finite. It is a precious commodity that should not be spent lightly.

You owe it to yourself to consider carefully the environment you create for yourself. It will have an irrefutable, positive effect on how you experience yourself, those moments of your existence. In the case of a prison cell, it is demeaning. In the case of your home, it should be affirming.

And if we do it right, we might have the chance to slow down time. Everything experiences change. Everything is in flux. We cannot stop it. Even your home will change day by day, season by season. The decomposition of matter will change it as well. It will change through your eyes, changed by your lived experiences. The better the design of your home, the bigger the chance to stop the constant churning of being. Good design has the power to arrest time. A building, a space well considered, has the power to hold an instance. For a short moment, it can hold time still.

It is therefore acceptable, even paramount, to appreciate the funds you invest in the quality of that time as money well spent. The better you do in the crafting of your home, the richer your time will be.

Van Life

In the summer before writing this book, my family and I rented an RV and traveled across the country and observed the hauntingly beautiful deserts, mesas, and canyons of the American Southwest.

During the stays on various campsites, we couldn't help but to wonder what a continued life on the road would look like. This was spurred on by the declaration of one of our daughters to cash in her chips for several years of van life—the process by which you upfit a random van with a mattress and other comforts of various degrees to take it on the road, freed of the conventional and sedentary life.

Studying our neighbors, ranging from teardrop trailers to multimillion dollar motorhomes, we checked out the market for these vehicles. The first question that arose was how to finance such an endeavor. After a little research, we found out that a motorhome is partially a vehicle and partially a home, and the financing of it is handled as a mixture between the two. This left us with a second question: How is it that cars depreciate and houses do the opposite?

After all, both the car and the house will wear down from too much love and use. Both require upkeep and service. Both will age out as far as the newest trends or technologies are considered, unless they are a collector car or a home that is considered to be exceptional. By all rights, there shouldn't be any difference in the monetary value consideration. You buy a shiny, new object and sell the worn-out, dull remnant for less. You rub off its life and pass on the leftovers.

After looking at it closer, it turns out both actually depreciate. In the case of the house, it can be said that it can increase in value if it sits in a parking lot that appreciates. Not that the dirt itself experiences any change in evaluation. Rather, we appreciate and value the land we build on with different eyes as the years move on and our collective love affair with certain parts of town change.

When it appreciates, or indeed depreciates as well, it is because of the aforementioned fads, weaponized prejudices, or economic shifts. An economically booming city will run out of space, will concentrate life in existing neighborhoods and build out new areas on its peripheries. It will shift and change its hot spots of real estate. The need for status will want us to rub the right shoulders. Or we might be driven by the establishment of new cultural centers, new locations of retail, school districts, and the quality of restaurants, or the proximity of just the right kind of coffee shop. When the arrows point up, our patch of land will grow in value; our homes on that land will not.

During the recent Great Recession, we learned that these value considerations can be flimsy and even are possible to evaporate.

If you go for a collector car or a home that is outside of the utilitarian norms, you will upend those forces. Money spent on lasting values will be returned. The need for happiness does not have an expiration date.

» Money spent on lasting values will be returned. The need for happiness does not have an expiration date. «

Pawns and Carcasses of Industrial Thrift

As I am lining up these disparate thoughts, these vignettes of a search for the true measures of a home and the happiness we seek, as well as the pressures to perpetuate the mediocre, I am left to wonder what kind of lobbyists wander the halls of Washington, DC. Or rather, what industries have tasked them to cement and buttress what must be the world's largest Ponzi scheme—or at the very least, quite a racket?

The houses we get to choose from are mostly shaped by the output of an economic system run by fast developers, industrial-sized builders, and hungry mortgage lenders. They are piggybacked and emboldened by innocent appraisers, realtors, and real estate attorneys, whose services are needed to run the machine.

Before I alienate all my friends, I should preface these words by saying not all fall into this generalization. The professionals in these industries I met and learned to trust over the years carry on, searching for something better, despite these headwinds.

We took a quick stab previously at how our houses come to be. Here is one way to expand on that particular riff. As a society, we push the idea of house ownership as an intrinsically all-American virtue. Developers and supersized builders buy up cow pastures and pepper them with empty square feet of gray carpet and beige walls. Mortgage companies step in to grease the wheel and slice up the interests in order to hawk them to the highest bidder. The only purpose of that process is the concentration of massive wealth for a precious few. The outcome is cold carcasses of industrial thrift that we are asked to nest our homes in.

We are sold on the idea of owning a house to build wealth, while we seldom do. Houses are actually owned by the banks. In turn, they install us as in-house custodians and free groundskeepers of their investments. It's quite a brilliant move, if you think about it. The bank invests into a piece of real estate, convinces us unsuspecting seekers of a home to move in, pay interest on the bank's investment, keep the investment in good shape, and, at the same time, pay for repairs out of pocket. Then they have us unload the investment prematurely after we paid most or all of the interest, returning the principal in full. The beauty in this scheme is that the unsuspecting homemaker is made to feel a responsibility to protect the bank's principal with their life.

Our municipalities are, of course, in on this deal. After this time and money is spent toward the margins of big corporations, any county can swoop in and take it all from us in case we cannot pay their share of the setup, the property tax. At a tax delinquent auction sale, we are left without a dime and without a home. They slap a bad credit rating on our profile after bankruptcy proceedings and kick us to the curb. After having paid everyone, we are left with nothing to our name. We have done our duty.

Even if we make it through the entire process unscathed, full ownership is bestowed to our name, and the value of our belongings has grown because of the ZIP Code reevaluation by our contemporaries, we will most likely have spent all that increase on interest payments and inflation in the meantime.

It is important for the upkeep of this machine that we repeat these steps and that the steady flow of uninspired houses is maintained. Through the multiple listing service (MLS) system and the support of unimaginative appraisers, the banks ask for assurances that the same house has just sold for the same price per square foot in the same ZIP Code. The fewer the differences, the safer the proposition. They are not in the business of selling you a home that is created in your interest. They are in the business of producing real estate-backed investments and installing us as quiet pawns to secure the deal.

There is almost no difference between you being a house owner or renting as an alternative. There will simply be another entity inserted into the setup—the landlord. You will still make the same payments, adding the extra margin for the landlord, who will in turn shoulder the ultimate risk for that payment.

To make it all work, we will need an endless increase in paying folks who are unsuspecting enough and fall for the lure of buying a run-of-the-mill house. Since there is a palpable limit to a sustainable increase in population, we also need them to yearn for ever larger entities. Bigger is better. Escalating consumption is the name of the game.

The flimsy cardboard boxes that are provided for us to live in are built to last for a decade. This is just long enough to meet any jurisdiction's requirement for those houses to stand up, protecting the building conglomerates. The reason houses have lasted any longer is because of the homeowners' constant and free input.

All of this blew up in 2008. The greed and gambling had ballooned to a degree that even the initiated wondered if this could hold up. The slicing up of the financial instruments and the number of hands wanting in on this racket had grown to mythical proportions. The massiveness of it all, of course, prevented it from imploding. A push of a button by the Federal Reserve and the whole thing got duct taped back together with made up funds. Afterwards, it was said that all these shenanigans had to stop. Naturally, a decade later all was forgotten and the game was back and bigger than ever.

I don't mean to offer these considerations as a half-baked conspiracy theory, but rather as an oversimplification of a massive and convoluted industry. My interest is for you to see the semblance of a larger picture against which you can make the right decisions so that you get to create a home for yourself that will serve you and you alone.

What are you left to do? First, realize that the common real estate metrics are for a circus that your considerations are not part of. If you are in for a true home that is created for you and only your interest at heart, then most likely a construction loan can cover only a portion of your cost. With enough surgical skill, the system can be bent to your benefit.

Frankly, I suggest you pitch a tent for the first few decades of your adult life and take the surplus funds and invest them into the very same companies that run the show. Buy up partial ownership of these companies. When you have built up enough cash reserves to fund your dream and are not bound to the vagaries of a heartless industry, fund your luxury on your terms and do as you please. The more you can pay for your home with your own hard-earned cash up front, the freer you are left to operate.

When We Hate

Over a couple of decades ago, as a student of architecture, I found myself on the top floor of a library in Charlotte, North Carolina. It was the white-glove section where the special collection and historical artifacts were housed.

I don't recall the research project that had brought me there. However, what I stumbled over in the process was eye opening. By pure chance, I found myself viewing redline maps by local financial institutions from a century ago.

These maps had been created to mark neighborhoods within the city of Charlotte that were deemed unfit for mortgage lending. They specifically called out certain ethnic groups. Among the areas marked were Black, Italian, and Irish districts. The banks had essentially distributed internal memos banning their mortgage lenders from offering loans to anyone without the proper racial pedigree. If you were Black, Italian, or Irish, they denied you a mortgage and thus the opportunity to buy a house. To own a house, you had to be of Anglo-White descent.

To own a house meant to live the American dream. It provided status and the opportunity to build wealth for yourself and your family. Real estate property is the means through which the American continent was usurped and divided up. If you owned land, you participated in the American experiment. In fact, until the 14th Amendment was added to the US Constitution, a half century prior to these particular maps, you had to own property (besides being male, White, and at least twenty-one years of age) to be allowed to vote.

House ownership allowed you to take part in and belong within the American people, and to pass on this self-understanding to the next generation.

An investment in a patch of dirt meant to build tangible wealth. It was a wealth that allowed for further opportunities and access to the means that set one up for a life supported and protected, with a leg up.

The opposite meant a continued struggle and added to the numerous headwinds faced by those who found themselves in the "wrong" minority.

The details and mechanisms behind the racial wealth divide and house ownership specifically have been brought to the forefront of America's collective conscience recently and spawned much research and commentary. The *National Geographic* magazine detailed, for example, how this very redlining has caused the density of Los Angeles' tree canopy to reflect the racial categorization of districts a hundred years ago. As a result, historically Black neighborhoods continue to boast a lack of trees, which in turn increases the difficulties of cooling homes.

Trees offer protection against the burning rays of California's summer sun. A house surrounded by trees needs less power to cool. A streetscape partially covered by trees absorbs and radiates less heat to pedestrians, drivers, and adjacent homes. This literally means if you live in one of Los Angeles' historically Black neighborhoods, you have to pay comparably more to cool your home. In addition, the lower generational wealth has rendered these houses less insulated. Many of these houses are simply too hot to live in, impossible to cool properly. All this accumulates to an increase in negative health effects and compounding personal and economic hardship.

This article was most impressive by showing, in a foldout, a cross section of the city's urban fabric along a major traffic artery leading from the affluent White neighborhoods to progressively more diverse and Black neighborhoods, with the trees consecutively thinning out.

When we hate, we hate well. And when we set up systems of ownership with degrees of access like this, it becomes easy to ask questions toward its viability. Not only has the industrialized and institutionalized apparatus of house ownership served only a few, being as such exclusive, it has also failed to provide livable surroundings; it being demeaning, demoralizing, and quite simply destructive. In real terms, we literally hurt people with the way we create the houses we live in.

Since the passing of the Civil Rights Act of 1968 and its Title VIII section commonly known as the Fair Housing Act, practices of discrimination in the housing market have become illegal. This includes the redlining of districts by mortgage companies.

Nonetheless, change churns slowly. As described in previous chapters, we assign monetary value to our homes in quite an arbitrary fashion.

It stands in absolutely no relation to what is important to us. And it remains unjust. The real estate market value of a house, and with it the wealth it provides to its owners, is largely based, as we have shown, on the neighborhood it is in and the square feet it can claim. Historically Black neighborhoods are, for the most part, on the bottom of the list. A house designed and built with no care and consideration is markedly less valuable in a historically Black neighborhood than the exact same house in a historically White and affluent area. The house is the same. The dirt it sits on is not. It still is appraised, in part, inadvertently or not, on racial terms.

These few thoughts are obviously far from any meaningful understanding of the racial wealth divide we are facing. Nor, and most definitely not, am I suggesting here a prescription for its remedies. Maybe these few considerations provide a quick look at the very real consequences of the systems we have set up and within which we operate. Hopefully, when you can see the framework surrounding the creation of your house, you can make meaningful decisions on how to meet it in particular.

For those of us who have the opportunity to think and act outside these parameters, we should not hesitate to do so. When you understand the creation of a home as the positive endeavor it can be and assign your efforts accordingly, you might be able to break through these shackles of our collective hate. Chances are, when you create a home with care and attention, and when you disregard the real estate parameters we have set up for ourselves, you will create a home that might bring about positive change, if by ever so slightly a step.

Footprints

In the same vein, I should mention our efforts to destroy our habitat. We are actively laying waste to the very environment we live in. With our eyes wide open, we find ourselves in the process of committing collective suicide. We know what we are doing and what we could change and yet, so far, we largely refrain from doing so. And we are running out of time.

The creation of buildings naturally plays its part. Forty percent of all greenhouse gasses emitted in the US are related to carbon production during the construction of buildings, their heating and cooling, lighting, and operation.[17]

If we were to change drastically the way we design, build, and operate our buildings, we could counteract our destructive efforts. There are already plenty of options to tap into. And yet we don't.

Here, too, I would like you to be aware of the larger framework within which your home will be created. If you are cognizant, you have the opportunity to make decisions that are not only right for you but also for all of us for a long time to come.

Efforts to change the way we actually build are underway and some are even easy to tap into as prospective homeowners. All of them try in various degrees to improve how we meet the site and optimize its potential, how we decrease the use of non-renewable energy and water during construction, how we change the means of operation and decommissioning of buildings, the use of building materials that are produced and transported with a reduced environmental impact, and the indoor air quality of our buildings.

These efforts all suggest that if we design and build better buildings from an environmental perspective, we build buildings of better quality and buildings that are better for us. To build green is to build better.

That is, if you see your attention going toward a sustainable effort in creating your home, you are feeding your own luxury. Money spent on green building efforts is money spent on your well-being, for you right now and for the generations following you.

Yet, only one-fifth of home builders report themselves as executing at least 90 percent of their buildings with some green efforts. The majority of those efforts are only oriented toward energy consumption, with a wide variation in the intensity.[18]

The use of solar panels washes away all sins. No matter how high the energy consumption is to operate your house because of poor design and inadequate quality in construction, if the energy used is renewable, who is to ask?

However, at the very least, it is a good start and a solution ready to implement. The quality of solar systems has markedly improved since the beginning of the 21st century. And the industry has matured to offer good and reliable services by local and regional companies. In short, today, as of the writing of this book, you could include a solar panel system for free. And we are currently at the cusp of not only breaking even, but benefiting financially from their installation.

Depending on the willingness of the power company hooked up to your house, it makes monetary sense to cover a majority—or in some places, all—of your electricity needs with solar power harvested through panels on the roof of your house. Designed right, the cost of the system can equal the savings shaved off your electric bill. If it is included in your mortgage, you can see your monthly payment increase for the cost of the system by the amount your electric bill decreases every month. Thus, with a stroke of a pen, you could reduce the size of your carbon footprint with no cost to you. Even better, as an added bonus, those monthly payments would go toward your equity and not the profit line of the power industry. By the time this book will be out of print, the cost of installing a solar system in your home is expected to drop even lower in relation to the cost of carbon-produced electricity, offering not only to be a wash, but to add dollars into your bank account. The power companies will be paying you in excess for the output the power plant on your roof is producing.

Of course, you and our habitat would benefit if we would simply design and build with quality in the first place. Consider the aforementioned visors to your windows to the south and reduction of windows to the west and east. Simply considering the orientation of your home and designing its openings to sunlight accordingly can reduce your energy consumption. Similarly, the toolbox of design considerations is chock-full of simple moves that will cut down on the wastefulness of the operation of your home. When it comes to lowering your energy bill, once you are living in your home, it means hard money in your pocket. As for considering our habitat, you can be effective at no cost to you. All you have to do is ask for it.

Ultimately, though, building right will cost you more. However, you can pick from a curve. Previously, I have commented about the cheapness of our building industry. When no one demands a better home, efforts toward it will be hard to find. As an example, one can argue that we essentially live in homes with windows wide open, homes that we simultaneously heat and cool. Our houses leak. And they leak extraordinarily. For relatively little effort, you can have your home sealed and insulated properly during the construction. It can then be checked with an air blower test, or by an inspector of one of many energy efficiency programs, such as LEED for Homes or Phius Passive House. Instead of heating and cooling your yard, you will be left to conditioning the interior of your home, as one should. Both your energy bill and your environment will thank you for it in the long run. In similar ways, you can up the quality of construction running from inexpensive to unaffordable, from effective to past the reasonable. All you have to do is ask for it and pick to your heart's desire.

Other efforts lie in the creation and the use of building materials. Concrete, alone, is responsible for 8 percent of all greenhouse gas emissions. The culprit here is the production method, a major by-product being carbon dioxide. Concrete is currently made out of sand, gravel, water, and Portland cement. The chemical process of creating that cement, which is effectively the grinding, heating, and cooling of limestone, currently releases carbon dioxide. For every ton of cement, one ton of CO_2 is going into the atmosphere. Not to mention the carbon energy used to run the process. Every year, four billion tons of concrete are used in the world. Changing the production methods will have an impact. The game to do so is called carbon capture.[19]

The idea is twofold. Create less carbon dioxide in the manufacturing process and capture excess CO_2 within the concrete itself. This will reduce the overall addition of greenhouse gasses to our atmosphere, the safety shield to our existence. Any effort to draw more CO_2 out of the atmosphere is an effort to bring the atmospheric cancer to a halt.

We not only have to stop adding, but we are tasked with taking back some of the carbon dioxide we have overloaded our atmosphere with. Our assignment is to find ways for negative emission.

You can, for example, put geopolymer concrete (a concrete made with an alternative to Portland cement), sometimes called green concrete, to use. It produces far less in CO_2 emissions and provides side benefits such as high insulation values and resistance to freeze-thaw cycles. Another, and one of the newest processes, aims at using CO_2 as one ingredient in the making of cement. By this means, carbon is taken literally from smokestacks and captured within the concrete as an essential part. You can already purchase concrete blocks made of carbon-captured concrete—a commonly used masonry unit within the house-building industry.

Another new trend is the use of engineered lumber instead of energy-intensive products, such as steel or concrete. Cross-laminated timber, for instance, uses wood pieces and adhesives to create structurally sound beams and slabs to span large distances. Not only is it less energy consuming to produce, it also uses a renewable resource—one that actively captures carbon. Trees are ready-to-go carbon-capture factories.

We have no choice but to tap into the vast possibilities of designing, building, and operating our homes differently if we want to preserve the place that allows for human life to flourish. There is no reason we shouldn't. What holds us back are the same encrusted and entrenched industries that fear a loss of marketplace, while far better means, methods, and products await. In the same way you are discouraged from building for your happiness, you are being kept from building for your wellness. Your home is made for your life to be better. So don't hold back, ask for it, and don't listen to the folks that say, "Well, we have always done it like that." Why listen if no good comes from it?

From the makers of buildings to the cost of construction, the financial mechanisms, to our systems of exclusion, and the environmental cost of our actions, hopefully this section of the book gave you a quick look at some of the major forces that shape your house and sometimes prevent you from doing what is right.

As a bottom line, when you create your own home, you should ask for what is right, for happiness to prevail first and foremost, and for well-being to be met with force and tenacity.

Be aware of the entire picture within which the creation of your home takes place and act with the best intention despite all the nonsensical headwinds you face. You are allowed to do it right. Nothing should hold you back.

» We have no choice but to tap into the vast possibilities of designing, building, and operating our homes differently if we want to preserve the place that allows for human life to flourish. «

Going for bliss

Examples and ideas
to help you reach the
luxury you seek.

A Roof

Understanding what is holding us back to follow our bliss, we are left to ask what else there is to consider in creating our homes. If some of these influences have had a negative effect on the places we have created for ourselves to house our lives, what can we do to do the opposite?

We looked at four building blocks, namely, structure, space, texture, and light and shadow. What else is there we can allow ourselves to look at to promise a better setting, a better catalyst, a better home for the lives we lead?

What would we find if we allowed ourselves to ask what it really takes to house ourselves? A bed? A roof over our heads? Temperature control? Some basic amenities for safety, comfort, preparing food, and cleaning our clothes? Probably. But those practicalities are not enough. We need a place we can come home to—our sanctuary.

For the home of my family, my wife asked me, if nothing else, to allow us to feel as a family that is closely knit. She asked for us to be reaffirmed that we not only belonged, but belonged together.

As it was, we enjoyed the presence of three daughters, each two years apart in age. While laying out some possibilities, an idea took hold that hopefully would just do the trick. How about we give each daughter their own room for privacy but allow them to experience simultaneously each other's presence? Could they hide away in the comfort of knowing their siblings surrounded them

We threw another aspect into the mix, the understanding that a simple room, enclosed by four walls, feels much more open, light filled, and spacious when it has windows on at least two of its sides. Naturally, we thought to up the ante and asked for windows on three.

So, we set about and laid out the three rooms in a pinwheel fashion, like three petals of a flower sticking away from each other in different directions. At the center, the pistil of that flower pattern, we placed three entry doors. The entry, size, proportions, and layout of each room were nearly identical, suggesting the lack of any hierarchy.

Each room was almost mundane in nature. However, by pinwheeling the three spaces around a central point, the volume of each was sticking out from the next. It provided each room with three sides exposed to the exterior, allowing us to place tall floor-to-ceiling windows in three directions. This simplest of moves turned these regular bedrooms into grand affairs.

Best yet, at the very tip of each room, each sister could walk up to one of the windows and look across, out, and back in at another sibling. Those windows were placed close to the corners so that privacy was retained. Looking across, you would only see a small corner of the adjoining space, enough to see the lights turned on and off and shadows of the others passing by. With no mechanical means, it made each sister aware of the next one, without necessarily directly seeing each other. Each one of them could hide in their room—and of course they would—but they could never really escape the reassuring presence of each other.

We also made sure to make those windows facing one another partially operable. It allowed the sisters to invite in fresh air and to also literally open up one room to the next. While they joked that they would hang clotheslines across to pass secret messages, they never ended up doing so. However, they did conceive of visiting each other on an adjoining roof, accessible from those connection points.

Of course, I hope to credit mostly, if not both of us parents, at the very least their mother, for instilling a strong sense of a family bond, simply through the quality of our daily interactions. Nonetheless, I cannot help but to think the design of their shared yet private spaces did its part. At the very least, it supported the very same efforts. That all three are a tightly woven bunch and equally fiercely independent is undeniable.

I think it also helped that the rest of the house created a stage for them to descend on for a uniquely interactive performance. The common living spaces forced us to engage, if ever so gently. And so, our daughters experienced a gradation between open exposure, the vague presence of the other sisters, and complete privacy.

And all of it had its repercussions. We could not help but to learn how to share space and functions and how to live together. It forced us to ask ourselves how to wrap family feuds into civility. And on the flip side, even when doors got slammed

Fig. 21: View from one room to the other at the Witte Home, 2017, Toby Witte.

and pure, unadulterated, temporary hatred was spewed about, the brooding could only last but for so long, until the lights next door were turned on and shined across with tentative apologetic steps.

These rooms made it difficult to turn a cold shoulder for too long. Someone was always looking at you, while at the same time someone also always had your back.

The home for these three sisters hopefully provided more than just a roof over their head. Hopefully, it encouraged the kind of genius loci, the presence of being, that truly spells "home."

» The home for these three sisters hopefully provided more than just a roof over their head. Hopefully, it encouraged the kind of genius loci, the presence of being, that truly spells 'home.' «

My Stuff

It is liberating to show up at the airport with one suitcase, preferably a carry-on, to fly off to the unknown, the next adventure. It turns out all your belongings actually fit in one bag. Walking into a hotel or rental in a faraway place with nothing but a few changes of clothes, toiletries, a charging cable, a passport, and a wallet reduces your existence to that of experience and curiosity. That's how life should always be.

The return trip can feel quite the opposite. Thousands of square feet stuffed with burdensome bits and pieces, leftovers of your life, await. They are accouterments accompanied with obligations and responsibilities.

When we moved into our new, intentionally designed home, we had to work ourselves through a long process of purging. Stuff wouldn't fit anymore. Something had to go. If we hadn't so much as looked at it for a year, it went to the curb. There simply wasn't any new storage awaiting it.

Boxes of screws, nails, knobs, and rivets were easily discarded, despite my insistence they would become useful someday. I could reduce the five pairs of old pants for yard work to one—the one that was usually used anyway. The hideous, hand-me-down chair molding over in the crawl space turned basement had been awaiting any reason—really—to walk off the premises. The twenty-year-old tennis rackets we would pick back up at some point only needed a stern talking to—let's stop lying to ourselves.

What was much harder, though, were the tchotchkes on which past memories tried to cling. How could I let go of the vase, ugly or not, that was given to us by a close relative who had since passed away? What about all the knickknacks that seemed to mean so much to us, vessels of lost rituals, Horcruxes of forgotten loves, flytraps for fleeting meanings? After all, those were the very essence of us. They reminded us of what made us who we were.

But we had no choice. It was simply a matter of prying all things out of our clutching hands. Eventually, we just had to relent.

For the interim of the construction of our new home, we moved into a rental house—even smaller yet. Naturally, we felt encouraged to rent a storage unit. On average, every American needs six square feet of these manifestations of unadulterated gluttony. They constitute a forty-billion-dollar-a-year industry.[20] Some trumpery we just couldn't say goodbye to. We packed it so tightly that for an entire year we couldn't get access but to the very front row of boxes. When we finally found ourselves in the new home and dug out the very last remnants of our past life, we learned we didn't even want or need any of those leftovers.

The entire exercise was a cathartic process. It felt as if a huge boulder was lifted off our shoulders. Freed of all the stuff, the keepsakes, all these items paid for with hard-earned money turned out to be just things—things no one needed. We were freed of it all—not only the bric-a-brac itself but also the need for hoarding. The chains of past consumption had held us down.

A life without all that burden turned into a life of curious adventures. We turned our sedentary presence into just another travel experience. Real life was out there to be explored. Inside the new home, we met up for rest and shared meals. It became our safe meeting place, the spot for respite. It was a place that protected and provided pause, unencumbered by any meaningless troubles—stress that led to more stress. We left the anxieties outside on the front stoop, past which we were meant to explore another day.

It also turned out the more precious items were not our actual memories. The vases vanished. The memories remained—those memories that were worth keeping or were triggered through conversations or random sensory moments at their own pace, their own need to rear their head. It turned out those knickknacks associated with people and places of former importance had been pressure points. They had forced their presence on us without being asked. They heaved memories onto our conscience constantly and unrelentingly. Even the most loved people in our lives did not ask for that much attention. The good stuff had turned stale, turning every day into Thanksgiving family get-togethers. It became too much real quick for even the most hardened soul.

We kept the camping gear, used once a year. We stored the air vent filters, cheaper by the pack of four. There was just enough storage given to make the daily routines function. We kept scarves and gloves for the wintertime and bathing suits for the summer. A bread maker? Why, oh why? We have an oven. A slow cooker? We have a pot and a stove. Skis? If we want to break our necks, we'll rent them. The bolt to repair the chair? It turns out the local hardware store is the best stocked storage for such things after all. A walk-in pantry? The next grocery store is five minutes away and offers more than what we could ever provide.

After half a decade of living in this home of sparse storage, the stuff tried to get back in and settle—naturally. For it to have any chance to stay, however, other stuff had to go. The price of such idiotic, shortsighted, and ravaging consumption became increasingly prominent with each trip to Goodwill. We no longer could hide this realization by hiding the things themselves.

And so we turned our need to spend on experiences instead—on to the making of new memories. We shortened the circle of consumption. Eat it before it enters the house, ride it with the use of a ticket so it won't park itself at your doorstep, listen to it elsewhere and take the dream to bed. We have been on vacation ever since.

We haven't been without denial, of course. I, for one, cut my stacks of books by half. I should get them from the local library, or if I could warm up to the idea, read them on the device in my pocket. I am working on getting rid of the last few, though I might have to add the one you are reading for a while. And we have kept the enormous dish to roast a turkey. But our retirement life better fits into that suitcase.

Surely everyone's version of an unburdened lifestyle will look different. But the most basic questions should remain. What is this home of yours for? And with the answer to that question, you will find what items are needed to make it work. If you get rid of the rest, you will invite ease and happiness.

The design of your home should then also breathe that understanding and help you stick to better habits. If you build storage, you will fill it. If your home feels easy, through its detailing, materials, and colors, you will be hard-pressed to clutter it up. If your home soaks in the daily mess on its own, into built-ins, niches, and shelving, it will stay serene without effort.

Your home should not ask for you to enter just to dust off the ball and chain. Your life is there to be lived. Chances are you only have one to try it out. Allow your home to be the trusting partner in the affair. And please, free yourself of all those bits and bobs that hold you back!

>> Surely everyone's version of an unburdened lifestyle will look different. But the most basic questions should remain. What is this home of yours for? And with the answer to that question, you will find what items are needed to make it work. <<

Good Design Is Simple

As part of the aforementioned home we created for our family, the issue of our front entry arose. The house, by nature of our own personal economics, had to be small. Yet we asked it to be excessive in its sense of spaciousness and to meet our own way of life purposefully. We asked for a lot and could only afford a little.

It meant every last function and quality of space had to be pared down to its utmost simplest manifestation. If less was more, we had no choice but to revel in it. We had to create richness with limited resources. The house had to work. It had to fit us, be a perfect stage for our lives, and also meet our budget.

As luck had it, the very process of simplifying a design is a recipe for success—for intrinsic beauty, functionality, and ease of use.

One of our particular ways of engaging with our home was, upon entering, to take off our shoes and shed our coats. And in this home, one was to be entering through the front door. It was to be the grand entry and utilitarian access all in one.

When five people enter—and three teenagers, large feet, and four seasons are involved—layers abound. Things were going to pile up.

So what to do? The process of making things look simple and easy is hard. You have to throw everything and the kitchen sink on the drawing board and then whittle away. Here we had a grand welcoming entry, a coat closet, shoe storage, a place to sit down and put on footwear, and a grand staircase ascending to the upper realms of our family life.

The end result was a four-by-five-foot foyer. That was it. Enough to swing the door open, hold the handle, and invite in a guest. How did it provide for all the rest? Easy.

The grandeur, for example, came from the brick wall I mentioned before (see page 92)—a linear element, rich in texture, starting far out at the exterior, leading you into the foyer and then up the stairs. The stairs, too, were considered with care. They were handmade by a good friend and fine woodworking master (see page 124). A warm material treated to a modern application, void of any protruding nosing at the treads and with edges exposed to the public spaces, flush with the wall below, and plenty of openness above. The surfaces of the treads and risers were of the same material and seamlessly continuous—a carpet of wood.

While a brick wall defined the entry space on one side, a glass front door on another, and a pristinely crafted staircase on a third, it was marked off by the remnants of a thick interior wall on the fourth. Enough of it was left to demarcate and partially hide the entry, while plenty of it was removed to let our guests spill past us and into the public spaces of our home, while we held the door.

As for the gazillions of shoes, we provided plenty of storage. Most of it went into flat, vertically arranged shoe cabinets that were let into the brick wall and finished flush with its surface—essentially, six-inch-deep cabinetry, the compartments of which fell open into the space and filled up a niche within the heavy masonry wall. If that wasn't enough, we opened up two of the bottom stair treads and gave them depth. Shoes slid under those steps, the heels of which were left exposed to the onlooker.

In order to put on those shoes, all one had to do was to sit down on the same treads that housed them.

Fig. 22: Entry shoe storage at the Witte Home, 2017, Toby Witte.

It should be said that the staircase was a straight run. And when approaching the house, the entire flight of stairs was visible through the front door, providing a backdrop when looking in from outside. Lights shined on the warm wood surfaces and created the effect of a cozy, welcoming entry, beckoning one into a friendly home.

And the jackets, you ask? Those were stored in a niche that was carved out of one of the heavy wall elements toward the living spaces. One step up on the stairs and you could reach for your coat that had been neatly tucked away from view. A small light inside the niche turned it into an elegant setup.

Had you removed all the items of footwork and clothing, the space would not have looked much different. Yet just enough of them, a few hints, livened and warmed up the space. They were, in fact, displayed as the items that accompany our lives, not intrusive, but yet a reflection of us. They managed, however partially hidden, to introduce a splash of color and personality.

All the elements that shaped the entry were simple in form and detailing and part of the infrastructure already in place. Just a few walls, a door and a staircase, each simplified in its massing and expression, hit the scene as proud performers. Yet, they were warm and rich in texture to profess an air of sophistication. They defined with simplicity a space that was complex in its functions.

It was a space also complex in its dynamics, as it yearned to flow into several directions—straight to enter and proceed up the stairs, sideways to expand into the living areas, and out toward the adventures awaiting.

Light and views were allowed in and guided to provide privacy, yet they also created a sense of openness and a playful personality as the day, weather, and seasons changed.

I sometimes joked that this entry was the biggest foyer a house had ever seen—even as you were hitting your elbows. Be that as it may, it was a joy finding simple and gentle solutions for each of the elements this entry had to handle.

If ever so humble, it tried to offer a suggestion about how good design needs to generate its own elegance from paring down its elements to what is necessary. Good design needs to make life easier, simplified, less burdened.

Just by showing up with ease, belying an innate complexity, good design removes the fussy and provides a chance for your life to unfold unburdened and inspired.

» If less was more, we had no choice but to revel in it. We had to create richness with limited resources. The house had to work. It had to fit us, be a perfect stage for our lives, and also meet our budget. «

Our Betrayal

If earlier chapters have not convinced you yet, the COVID-19 pandemic should have made it painfully clear—we loathe to live in our homes. Our homes have failed us. Or maybe we have failed them. They simply don't work. At the start of the pandemic, home improvement projects, backyard upfits, and additions had steadily increased in number and were projected to continue to rise.

This comes to no one's surprise. We had been asked to spend the entirety of our time at home in order to hide from each other. Unable to flee to other places such as work, restaurants, and shopping malls, we had been cooped up and forced to admit our existing houses have failed to provide us with livable surroundings.

Divorces had risen by over 30 percent during the beginning of the pandemic.[21] I will refrain from blaming all our social and interpersonal failures on the quality of our built environment, but these dots are just too impressive not to be connected.

Instead of cuddling up during the pandemic in the warm embrace of a home, we had to create a life within the empty, heartless boxes that our building industry had produced. Our engagement with our houses intensified and we got to see firsthand how these crops of mass production had let us down. They had been barely good enough to fall asleep in, drowse our psyche with endless episodes of our favorite TV shows on the latest streaming service, and shovel in a bowl of cereal before running off to somewhere else. Before the pandemic, we had tried to be anywhere but home. To live in them now full time was a lot to ask for.

At home, we found our loved ones and ourselves, both painfully too close. To be by ourselves or to be with our life partners takes special considerations. There are times when we engage and times when we need to hide. Too much of a good thing can be simply too much.

A true home should be able to provide the right kind of spaces for the tasks, emotions, and moments our lives generate. This means we should not offer a confluence of simple cells, rectangular rooms with four walls and a door, for each instance of being. Instead, our lives ask for pockets, niches, and areas, spatial definitions that can range from the most ephemeral to the very specific. They should range from the most public to the most private. They should vary in size, materials, colors, intensity of natural light, views, access, transition, flexibility, and more.

Picture, for instance, a huge farm table, large and robust enough to seat twelve or more people, made of heavy planks of weathered and worm-holed solid oak. A bench of the same material is along one side, chairs of various kinds everywhere else. Picture this as a center for your own family life, whomever that might include. It sits in the middle of a light-filled space, airy and open. You come here to engage. It's the public forum of your nucleus group of loved ones; added on to occasionally by outside relatives or close friends. It's safe enough to test out truth bombs, to ridicule, love, hate, and hang out together. You are in the safety of your home while at the same time being exposed to each other. If you prop up your laptop here, it is with the understanding that you will be interrupted. In fact, you show up here to interact, not to be alone, with all the good and bad the presence of the ones closest to you brings. This space is looking inward on to the island of the table. This is the consummate stage for your interaction.

Now say you feel the need to disengage for a while. You need a break, maybe to read a book or enjoy a glass of your favorite drink by yourself. Let's say we offer to you the opportunity to scoot behind an open wall that disengages a narrow little pocket adjacent to the main congregation area. It might be just large enough to hold one comfy chair and a side table, or a shelf on a wall. Maybe it's surrounded on two sides by nothing but glass with fantastic views of nature. The separating wall, heavy out of stone, stops just enough to render the enclosure incomplete. There is no door, just an opening. You are close enough to hear the boisterous engagement of your loved ones, enough to feel the comfort of knowing they are nearby. However, you are separated and turned into a singular and opposite experience. Here you snuggle up by yourself and are allowed to let your gaze venture far. This space is barely enough to encompass your presence. It certainly will ensure you are left alone. It is peaceful and turns your attention either inward or to the vast exterior. The world here is inhabited by you alone. Only the perking up of your ears might appreciate the proximity of others. You are not locked up, though, behind closed doors. All it takes for someone to get your attention is to peek around the wall. But most likely, your loved ones should feel they ought to knock on something to mark the disturbance. This space is clearly meant for you alone at that moment. It is hardly large enough to allow for a room tag with a name on a floor plan. But powerful it is—as powerful as it is specific and rare.

In this kind of manner, each quality that your life provides and asks for should be met in subtle but intentional design moves so that your home can be lived in with ease. Our lives and our relationships are complex. They ask to be met with specificity and empathy. A true home comprises a potpourri of spaces that can playfully respond to your changing moods, the complex dynamics of your close interpersonal relationships, your shifting daily routines, and ever-reinventing pastimes.

The pandemic also asked us to get used to the new world of video calls. The simple act of working from home should not have taken more than a bit of desk space, one might think. But it turns out our minds enter a different universe when switching from our private life to work life. Meeting a "Brady Bunch" group of people on our computer screens meant we had to turn on our extrovert avatars. We had to do so in the middle of our own private sanctuary. We allowed strangers to enter our homes, the one place where all pretenses fall and we are at our most vulnerable naked self. Suddenly, the screaming kids were an embarrassment and our partner scurrying by in their unmentionables too much for the outside world to witness. We had to realize that the switch from our public persona to our private one is not an easy one to make.

An entire new expectation was hoisted onto our home. It became a forum for daily public engagement. Our incredulity of the failure in this only serves as testimony to how little we understand the needs we have in our home, let alone the ability to respond to them.

We could lie to ourselves before the pandemic. We could drown any inkling of displeasure and stark realization of failure by turning on our screens, the portholes to make-believe, better worlds. We could avoid living for too long in our own realities. Stuck at home for good, forced by the COVID pandemic, it became impossible to keep up the charade. For those of us who could, we threw money at it. We built another room to our house, or an outside pool to throw the kids in. When that didn't work, we filed for divorce.

None of this is necessary if we allow ourselves to pay attention in the first place and design our houses properly. When we create a home with specificity, empathy, and ingenuity, chances are they will not only work well, they will even enhance the life we seek. Our homes should be our own oasis of bliss.

Fig. 23: Reading spot at the Gerendák Residence, 2022, Toby Witte.

Good Design Is Innovative

Throughout the next three chapters, I will try to showcase several distinct design ideas we allowed ourselves to play with in a single project, the Gerendák Residence.

The quality of structure we discussed previously (see page 75) came about as we contemplated a very specific wish from our clients. They had asked to be provided with cantilevers jutting out of the hillside overlooking a lake.

Part of the consideration included their plans to live in their home into old age, a time when climbing stairs might be an issue. To solely rely on mechanical means to hoist them high onto a platformed space by elevator seemed risky.

After contemplating these and the rest of the programmatic requirements for a while, we found a solution. We cut a terrace into the hill, not unlike a mountainous rice paddy, with the help of a set of one-story-high stone walls. Essentially, we created an artificial cliff. On the edge, we could then teeter several volumes of the home that could careen out into thin air. Our clients could enter these volumes on one side on ground level and look out at the other from a vantage point in midair.

We picked three primary spaces that seemed to beg the most for these views: the main bedroom suite, the living area, and a studio space.

Not stopping there, we wondered whether we could invite three different treatments to the act of cantilevering.

The first followed a straightforward two-thirds rule, by which we anchored the entire bedroom as a simple box into the mass of the house with two heavy steel beams. One-third of those steel beams stuck out over the edge of the cliff and two-thirds into the structure of the house sitting on the terrace.

The second was created out of the complex, yet simple, set of wood beams described before. It housed the living area and blurred the demarcation from solid ground to precarious floating, from inside to outside. Like the Roadrunner running from his archnemesis and finding himself suspended in midair, this treatment allowed our clients to venture from the kitchen to the sitting area and on to a terrace, not quite realizing where the inside stopped and the outside began. Walls started out as solid and ended as nonexistent. And the floor crossed from supported to hovering without a clear threshold.

The third, however, was one that even surprised us. The studio space was a separate building volume, connected to the rest of the house only by a narrow glassed-in breezeway. It was to be an office space to begin with and to offer the option to turn into a separate full suite with a bathroom and kitchenette later in its lifetime. The footprint measured thirty by eighteen feet. In height, it filled out sixteen feet. We treated it as an elegant elongated box, simple in its appearance and intricate in its detailing. Just a pristine object from the exterior and an exquisite space from the inside.

Structurally, it came with an enormous problem. The studio was sitting with only a short portion on the hillside terrace. Imagine placing a birthday present, boxed up in a neat long parcel, onto a table and pushing it over the edge long past the point at which it can resist the demands of gravity.

Breathtaking were the views in three directions as one stepped over the edge, off the cliff, and toward the edges of the studio. However, somehow the box needed to be held up.

A true cantilever was not an option here to support the flying end of this building. Placing a few simple posts underneath would rob the whole setup of a sense of precarious weightlessness. Once you land an airplane on its wheels, it transforms from a magical flying contraption into a car. Once you place columns under an overhanging structure, it no longer functions as a cantilever. More importantly, it no longer looks and feels as one.

We decided on what the homeowners eventually came to call lovingly a "set of chopsticks." We pierced two round steel poles through the box and into the ground at two disparate angles. Shooting off in different directions, the opposite of plumb, they moved from the periphery of the structure. They poked into the built space and out through the roof. They were uncomfortably thin, and visible from all sides as well as the interior. Those chopsticks acted structurally as posts, but visually as independent elements that were doing anything but holding something up.

We gave the Roadrunner unreasonably long stilts that allowed him to stay in his lofty spot for the long pregnant minute before he realized he should be, by all accounts of modern science, in total free fall. Against all odds, the cantilever that wasn't, and the posts that weren't, kept the studio among the treetops.

To call this an innovation of high measure might be far-fetched. However, we took apart a problem and asked to see the experiential qualities we sought and the structural systems needed for what they were. We took apart a thing, looked at its components with a clear appreciation, and reassembled it in the way it asked for.

Arguably, part of what any design process ought to offer is this very opportunity of revelation, steps through which we strive to see with fresh eyes—to find new answers and to ask new questions.

In the creative act, we are allowed to take a problem or requirement and disassemble it into its parts, hoping to find new connections, new expressions, new functionalities, and new qualities.

Fig. 24: Chopsticks of the Gerendák Residence, 2022, Toby Witte.

The result, of course, will offer the potential for wonderment. It will provide for a discovery that will allow you to see the exceptional in the mundane.

Good Design Is Specific

If wanting to be suspended in thin air was a specific wish from our clients, the baby grand piano pushed itself onto the stage with some aplomb.

Music was an integral part in the life of our clients and so we took it literally and placed it in the center of the building. While the cantilevers elevated the primary spaces of repose, the music room became the organizing element for the circulation and the functions of the home.

In fact, it became the nucleus out of which the entire house grew. We began by understanding the dynamics of the sound within this tiny cell and through it the geometry and detailing of the space. We then followed up by wrapping it with functions and spaces just like the layers of an onion.

As a result, the music room received a heavy sound-buffering shell of complex built-ins, while all surrounding spaces retained a relationship with it through their proximity and connectivity. All daily movement circulated around and through this core area, both in plan as well as vertically. Even the lower floor, reserved for guests, picked up the geometry and orientation toward this room above and was connected by the floating staircase that, if so desired, became part of the musical core.

In two directions, the space for the piano opened up with room-high sliders to the main living area and, by way of the adjoining staircase, to the downstairs. The onion layers could peel partially back. By a push of two panels, the music could fill the entire home for the purpose of entertainment, and portions of the magnificent views were provided to the musician. Conversely, the space could be closed off for private and tentative practice.

Whether the piano was being played or stood silent, its presence was felt throughout the house with this acoustic and spatial treatment. Like a beating heart, it reliably pulsated at its center. Even guests were guided past it first, to allow it to stake its claim upon their consciousness. It was to be known that without the sound of music or the mere possibility of it, there would not be a home. The music came first, the home and the habitation second.

It goes without saying that for any design to be successful, it has to be generated from within. A specific need has to be answered. The process of design has to be intentional, even while it allows for the serendipitous to happen, in order for us to form a meaningful relationship with it. In the case of the Gerendák Residence, music was not only to be provided a stage, it was to become the connecting thread, without which the home would be rendered lifeless. Through the music and the piano, we had found a key into the life of our clients and the home was asked to respond to it, piece by piece.

When we ignore the specific, we will find ourselves with formal dining rooms no one uses or empty guest rooms we maintain, both of which excel in nothing but collecting dust.

If, instead, when designing our home, we find ourselves to be specific about our way of living, our own memories, desires, and aspirations, we create the chance for magic to happen.

Fig. 25: The music room of the Gerendák Residence, 2022,
Toby Witte.

It might not have been by chance that, throughout the design process, the piano showed up as a shape in plan akin to that of a heart.

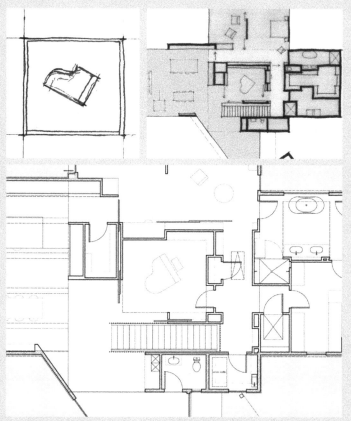

Fig. 26: The music room of the Gerendák Residence
in various stages throughout the design, 2022, Toby Witte.

Good Design Is Poetic

For magic to happen when we inhabit our homes, the most important ingredient might be the poetics of it all. And that, of course, is quite an elusive quality to strive for. You will know, however, you have succeeded when you feel goose bumps trickling down your spine and your heart skipping a beat.

The creation of your home will be concerned with a myriad of practical matters. Everyone involved will be occupied with specifics, the how and when of every last piece. From the moment you are considering the idea of creating a home for yourself to the first morning waking up in it, the questions will mostly focus on the mundane. That's how many of us are, if not wired, then trained. Nonetheless, we want someone or something to place a finger on our chest, right at the location of our heart, look at us, and say "you," so that we feel warmth washing through our system. Yet, we will try to get there by engaging our mind and unique faculties to form abstract thought. "Make me happy. Make me whole," turns into step one and then step two.

And so we must. The design team will contemplate zoning designations, building code guidelines, and construction methods. The builder will arrange subs, costs, and timelines, and the plumber will figure out where to obtain the coupling and how to attach it. You will find yourself asking whether the refrigerator has side-by-side doors, how many kilowatts per hour the solar system will spit out, and how many keys you will end up with. And of course, all of that has to happen.

When it's all said and done, however, the purpose of it all is to indeed supersize your bliss. The entire exercise is there for one purpose—to make you ecstatic with happiness. Your home is there to bring joy to your life. That is it.

All the rest can be provided without even living in a home that is yours. So, we must always keep the end goal in mind throughout the process. While we have to allow ourselves to go down each and every rabbit hole and become specific, we always have to make ourselves return to daylight and remember what the exercise was for.

In the end, you will remember none of the details your or everyone else's mind had been concerned about. All you will do is fall into the embrace of your home, cuddle up in its lap, and fill the stage that it provides for your own life. Your happiness will not be burdened by any zoning restrictions thereafter.

The Gerendák Residence was chock-full of moments that tugged at our clients' heart strings. It succeeded in showing up simultaneously grand and cozy. The most powerful gesture it might have offered was found in its relationship to the surrounding trees. Both inside the living area with its tall and vast glass facades or out on the cantilevering terrace, it took you flying high among the trees' tall trunks and green tops. Exposed to powerful and breathtaking nature with naked immediacy, it held you back safe and sound in its caring embrace.

It is difficult to describe how this home met the homeowners personally and specifically. It is easier to share the instance of the general contractor taking a couple of curious visitors on a tour during the construction of the home. He shared how uncomfortable he became when they literally exclaimed with joy, moving from space to space with tears running down their cheeks. While it wasn't theirs to be, they had found a place that felt like home.

An even easier example is the development of the staircase connecting the main living quarter on the upper floor with the guest wing below.

Staircases are a special breeding ground for the technical to grow stubborn. They are laden with building code restrictions. An average of more than a million patients annually have been treated for stair-related injuries in US emergency rooms in recent years.[22] Our response has been to formulate the most specific guidelines for their geometry, consistency, and enclosure.

Part of it is the staircase's unique role to force us moving vertically, an act that feels instinctively unnatural. It is also a clumsy and thoughtless way with which to connect two distinctly separated realms of spaces. Mostly because of the economics of construction, we continue to stack separate levels of a house on top of each other, disengaging them as abruptly as possible.

We are prone to search for the horizon line. Craning our necks and looking upward is not our specialty. The relationship of spaces to each other is harder to appreciate when they are thoughtlessly heaped on a pile.

Last but not least, it requires appropriate and therefore costly labor and materials to create a set of stairs (see page 121). All to be said that a stairway is handicapped to begin with, retaining nothing remotely resembling a moment of poetry.

Naturally, we tried anyway at the Gerendák Residence. To do so, we looked at two distinct parts of the problem: the quality of space and detailing of materials.

As for the space surrounding the steps, we increased its complexity, letting it slip, slide, spill, and swirl in every which direction. We worked to infuse it both with vertical and horizontal expressions, and everything in between. In effect, we tried to provide a space for the stairs as a leftover happenstance and confluence of many different formal elements.

On one side, for instance, we leaned the stairwell against an exposed, strong stone wall that spanned two floors. It was part of the terracing described before and experienced on the interior and exterior alike. Opposite, we exposed the plane separating the two levels, allowing a view of both floors and their separation from each other. Traversing the stairs, one was to engage with the music room, the foyer, and grand living room upstairs.

Fig. 27: The top of the staircase with a view toward the entry at the Gerendák Residence, 2022, Toby Witte.

This allowed for viewing spaces delineated by a mosaic of disparate elements ranging from sliding panels, screens, and wood beams to solid walls and changing ceiling heights. Downstairs, the space washed sideways into a lobby-like area, a seating space for both guest rooms that opened in two directions toward views of the lake. Besides manipulating the space and treating it as a playful body of water, half quirky stream, half waterfall, we also tried to provide vantage points of distinct quality for one's eyes to focus on when engaging with the stairs. In many ways, we tried to make it all about anything else but the stairs themselves.

Hand in hand with the shaping of the space, the detailing of the materials forming treads, raisers, handrails, and balustrades was also carefully considered. Here, too, we tried to take apart the pieces, creating the staircase. For instance, we let each tread float independently, neither touching anything on their sides nor each other. Slabs of solid wood were placed floating in midair, supported only by a single, sloped steel beam running down the center of the path.

To prevent people from falling off the side where the space opened up, we introduced screens of vertical

Fig. 28: Staircase of the Gerendák Residence, 2022, Toby Witte.

metal rods, spanning from floor to ceiling on both levels. We essentially provided a stout barricade for reasons of safety, while dissolving it to its smallest possible physical manifestation. Each rod vanished cleanly into a floor on one end and a ceiling on the other. As a group, they formed a mere wisp of a barrier, a nearly nonexistent presence of being.

Overall, as a result, it seemed as if all the areas surrounding the stairs were included into the entire ensemble—from top to bottom and left to right. The stairs themselves appeared light and elegant, gently falling into a spot left by walls and ceilings pushing in all directions.

Not only was movement itself transformed into an exquisite sculptural setting, it was offered to develop into a ballet performance of moving bodies, flowing spaces, divergent physical elements, and a rich material palette. Once construction was finished, windows cleaned, and lights turned on, the entire performance was rendered alive.

To scale these stairs was to be poetry in motion. The ordinary act was transformed into a moment of beauty.

» When it's all
said and done,
however, the
purpose of it
all is to indeed
supersize your
bliss. The entire
exercise is there for
one purpose—to
make you ecstatic
with happiness.
Your home is there
to bring joy to your
life. That is it. «

Good Design Is Sensual

I was recently invited to serve as a critic in a university's school of architecture. Students shared their work on a design project in order to receive helpful feedback. As a group, they had pinned up their individual drawings and 3D renderings and were sharing some images on a screen. In addition, they had built small study models, explorations of their ideas in rudimentary built form.

They had worked on this project for over a month and were still in a preliminary stage. While they were designing a true building, the work was meant to develop design processes and understandings, critical thinking skills, and the steps and methods necessary to work through a design problem.

But it was clear that the most exciting part for them was the design development of the building itself. And the drive among them all was to take a stab at one of many current design trends and to replicate the work of one star architect or another.

I tried my best to follow their thoughts and design work and to offer meaningful suggestions as best I could. I must have repeated one particular concern one too many times, for one student flagged me down during a break and asked me to expand on my point.

Most of the work had come off as what you might call "paper architecture," ideas that look good on paper, but seemed to fall flat as a building that would be engaged with in real time. By trying to emulate the work of others, they had failed to think of their buildings as actual built architecture. What might look good on paper does not always provide for a meaningful experience in built form.

The student who had stopped me said she didn't fully understand what I had meant and hoped to get a better insight. Not sure how to get to the point, I suggested that design should be sensual. Seeing her look of incredulity, I followed up by asking her to draw a cube.

By now, she was sure I had completely lost my marbles. But I egged her on. She didn't have a pen, so I gave her mine and a piece of paper.

With another supportive nudge on my behalf, she relented and drew a simple axonometric cube with nine simple lines, surely regretting ever having asked me in the first place.

When she was done, I asked her to pick it up. This, of course, robbed her of the last shred of confidence in my sanity. But I still insisted she grab it. I ended up suggesting she close her eyes and imagine the process of reaching out with her hand, touching the cube, feeling it, and picking it up.

While I was wondering if I had crossed any legal or ethical lines, she decided to be a good sport and humor me. Or maybe she had figured giving in to my nonsense would be the safest way to retreat. I thanked her by peppering her with more questions. I wanted her to commit to it, so I asked her about its size and weight, whether it was cold or hot to the touch, whether she could hold it in one hand or two, and how the surface felt. Slowly, she warmed up to the exercise and described the cube in her own terms. It began to feel real to her.

She described a cube that was about the size of a fist, quite dense and heavy, with a smooth polished surface. She described it as made of a solid metal that had been heated to a hot, glowing, lava-like state, just to be freeze-shocked into its present form. She vividly described the sensation of feeling that former red-hot state still pulsating from its core, if not in temperature, by way of some kind of innate energy—a sensation that caused her fingers to tingle and sent shivers up her arm.

"There it was," I suggested. At that moment, the cube had become real. Even though it was only existing in her imagination, it had turned into an object as real as the piece of paper she was holding.

Whether the cube would be actually made into a real form or not, it was alive. It existed. That was what I was missing from the designs I had perused before. I suggested to her that when she had experienced the cube in her imagination at that moment and had changed it based on that realization of the cube, if she had drawn it up again, it would have felt completely real to her. It would also have felt real in its depiction. Or rather, the realness of the cube would have emanated from the paper. And when it had, I would have appreciated it as real too.

When she had a sensory relationship with her design, it would become real. When it was real to her, it would be real to me. I offered that the way we appreciate our built environment is through that very sensual engagement she had experienced in her imagination.

When we design a building, the primary concern is not to simply push a few lines around in a floor plan to mitigate programmatic demands. Nor do we blindly copy visual excitement for its own good alone. Instead, we try to visualize built forms that have a chance to grab the ultimate inhabitants or users in a visceral and personal manner.

Drawings or renderings simply hold those moments in place before they vanish in front of our eyes. Through the design process, we try to generate surroundings that claim nothing less but to have the power to engage with us on a most personal level. By playing with our senses and emotions, we task them to generate a physical response. They should make us wonder and yearn. They should tug at our core. They should feel like a lover's first touch. They simply ought to be intoxicating.

There have been plenty of tales about how the paintings of Mark Rothko have moved people to tears. Some of his nondepictive, large-scale canvases emanate an energy that elicits an immediate emotional response. Just the layering of the color, the colors themselves, the texture, something about the application of it all, urges us to connect with ourselves in a fundamental way.

When our eyes touch the canvas, the paint, the ridges, the distortion of light, we are prompted by the contemplation of ourselves. We begin exploring questions, answers, and probing realities that can be too large to handle. These paintings allow us to relent to a purely human experience. We get to fall into our being.

That is the kind of power good design needs to aspire to. Our homes need to be given the chance to be sensual affairs. We deserve no less. Good design should urge us to want to engage with it. To touch it, feel it, be embraced by it.

By exploring these sensations in the design of a home, we are forced to appreciate every aspect in detail. It will cause us to pay attention and consider the materiality and texture of any element, be it a wall, structural piece, or the space itself. It will ask of us to consider the play of light and shadow, and to probe our expectations, dreams, and desires. It will provide us with a path to see the luxury we seek for what it is.

» Our homes need to be given the chance to be sensual affairs. We deserve no less. Good design should urge us to want to engage with it. To touch it, feel it, be embraced by it. «

The Wedding Planner

Good advice for a couple about to get married is to engage in premarital counseling. Rather than preventing them from the madness of their particular commitment, the idea is to dismantle some preconceived notions, to address their particular and individual motivations, to provide each the opportunity to raise pressing topics of shared life, and to allow each to speak freely. The basic goal here is, as with any good help or therapy, to explore the true nature of one's desires and the realities one might face. In this instance, the couple should openly talk about money, sex, gender roles, kids, how and where to live, etc.—the list is long.

The therapist functions as the neutral arbitrator and facilitator. Their sole interest is to ensure the couple dives into the journey, aware of their own and each other's expectations and the awareness that their particular needs could be met in new ways they might not have yet considered.

The concept of premarital counseling might be a new consideration. What isn't new is to involve a wedding planner for the ceremony.

When considering the following process, try to draw the parallels to the idea of creating your home.

Let's say the wedding planner provides you with three packages. The first being the bare-bones, nuts-and-bolts list of basics. Dress: check. Venue: check. Food: check. Photography: check. The next option includes more choices—a bit of handholding and guidance—about exploring why exactly you are asking for a wedding with two hundred guests, when, in truth, you are a very private person and your parents and your one friend are the only people that matter. The last option, the concierge service, perfectly balances your need for involvement and the pleasure of not having to worry about the minutiae being addressed and taken care of.

The wedding planner themselves do not function as the priest, civil servant, dressmaker, cook, or photographer. But they guide everyone, including you, to achieve the goals being explored, understood, and set up at the beginning. A wedding has the claws to shred your sanity to pieces without an experienced pilot on board.

You most likely agree that you would happily pay for these services, whether it is the premarital counseling or the wedding planning.

As the aforementioned relates to the creation of your home, the truth is that many "marriages" have failed during the process. This is precisely because prospective homeowners do not explore their motivations. They lack the right precedents, examples, and options to choose from. They are burdened by ill-fitting, preconceived notions and outside pressures. And they don't find an experienced and kind ear to vent, explore, discover, and craft a path forward that is right for them.

It is easy to be confused by the need for status or a family member's acceptance when asking for the biggest house on the block, when really you are asking for an exquisitely crafted surrounding that is measured by how it meets your life and provides a truly fertile ground for happiness. It is easy to only ask for the options you have experienced so far, provided by a quite limited and particular outlet, instead of exploring a vast set of possibilities beyond anything you have been allowed to consider before.

Those industry players that make money from your dreams finance most wedding magazines. And they sell you a very narrow slice of options in the process. It means more money for them and fewer answers for what you really need and ask for. This is especially true when you don't quite know how to ask the right questions.

When you create your home, if nothing else, ask for that exploration, help, and guidance. First, understand yourself and what your needs, restrictions, and dreams truly are. And explore what possibilities and options are out there. Understand the game, set the goalpost, agree on the rules, and then go wild, playing the game to the extent you see fit. Your happiness will be for the better.

The Luxury of You

———————

I hope that in the pages of this book you found an affirmation for a richness that provides a tantalizing ease to your life—a certain comfort, simplicity, and poignancy—that seems to be truly fleeting, yet tugs on an eternal desire. I hope I allowed you to yearn for a built environment that, as much as it slows down time for you, invigorates you. I hope you have seen a glimpse of how your home could be created with deliberation and intent, freed of meaningless market forces and preconceptions, freed of unnecessary burdens and superfluousness, and enriched with perhaps quieter and pregnant specificity. I hope I left you with a sense that you are tasked with asking for less stuff in order to receive a home that can positively engage with your senses, your emotions, and your probing mind.

I hope I illustrated why I think you will be set up well to find happiness in your surroundings if you heed these few simple suggestions in creating your own home.

- Start with a Clean Slate

- Ignore the Real Estate Metrics

- Ask Yourself What You Are Looking For

- Understand You Are Asking for Art

- Love the Process

Hopefully, I was also able to excite you about the potential for your own personal bliss that can be invigorated through four simple areas of attention and appreciation. Please remember that these qualities of your physical surroundings, if considered properly, have the power to lift your spirit, calm your nerves, provide comfort, offer a sense of safety, and continuously support your own sense of self.

- Structure

- Space

- Texture

- Light and Shadows

I hope I empowered you not to feel any pressure to follow footprints not worth following. We have grown accustomed to systems and methods that should be reversed and countered. Just because they have come to be does not make them necessarily worth being accepted. Please feel strength in your understanding of the arena in which you play and the clear vision with which you can succeed despite it.

Be aware of the entire picture within which the creation of your home takes place, and act in your interest despite all the nonsensical headwinds you face. You are allowed to do it right. Nothing should hold you back.

And last but not least, when you engage to create a true home for yourself, I hope you will ask for a home that will excel in the following. For I know that if you solicit these understandings, your home may provide an enriching stage for your life for years to come. Please trust that good design needs to be:

- Intimate

- Empathetic

- Simple

- Innovative

- Specific

- Poetic

- Sensual

And, if nothing else, please close this book believing that if you create your home with honest consideration, it will supersize your bliss.

Just remember, if a space you set out to create from scratch does not lift your soul, you haven't given it the attention it asked for.

As a parting thought, I would like to add that at the very center of the process of shaping a home is the creative act. While everything else about the design and construction can be optimized for the best possible outcome, the creative moment remains an elusive beast. You have to allow for the serendipitous to happen. You have to allow for discovery and to be swept off your feet. One cannot optimize bliss. But one can try to arrange for bliss to happen. And then some.

Thank You

I greatly appreciate that you stuck it out to these final lines. Hopefully, some of my rambling has stirred a new consideration or forgotten memory and allows you to appreciate your surroundings in a new light.

I would love to hear your feedback. If you go to www.supersizingbliss.com, you can sign up to receive email updates and additional information.

You can also reach me at toby@supersizingbliss.com for a personal follow-up. Please stay in touch.

If I have stirred your curiosity enough, please leave a review on Goodreads or Amazon or wherever the option is provided.

Acknowledgment

A big thanks to all the people involved in the making of this book. Your interest, support, input, ideas, feedback, advice, knowledge, expertise, and discussions have proven invaluable. Also, a big thank you to all of you who have joined in my journey over the past decades and who helped try to create homes that might have the chance for bliss to be elevated. There are too many of you to list here. You know who you are. I thank you.

About the Author

A quarter century of experience in the world of design and construction comes to bear on Toby Witte's work. Born in Peru, German by heritage and upbringing, Toby has had the privilege to study architecture, building science, drafting, and construction in Germany and in the USA.

Between various employments with architect, engineering, and construction firms, he graduated cum laude from the School of Architecture at the University of North Carolina.

He ran his previous design/build companies, Dialect Design and Qubell for over a decade, until he founded Wittehaus in 2017.

In 2004, he received the Henry Adams Medal and Certificate of Merit by the American Institute of Architects. And in 2018, he came in third for the People's Choice Award of the North Carolina Modernist Residential Design for the George Matsumoto Prize.

To learn, grow, and contribute, Toby has been an active member of the American Institute of Architects, the National Organization of Minority Architects, Brick & Wonder, EntreArchitect ASG Mastermind, and the German American Chamber of Commerce.

When Toby parks his pencil, he lets himself be sucked in by a vibrant family life centered on his wife, an early education teacher, and their three powerhouse daughters. He cooks, reads, travels, plays two chords on the guitar, and loves a good beer.

Endnotes

1   US Department of Commerce, 2015, https://www.census.gov/construction/chars/pdf/ c25ann2015.pdf; Evan Comen, "The Size of a Home the Year You Were Born," 24/7 Wall St, May 25, 2016, https://247wallst.com/special-report/2016/05/25/the-size-of-a-home-the-year-you-were-born/

2   US Census Bureau, Current Population Survey, Annual Social and Economic Supplements, 1940 and 1947 to 2021. https://www.census.gov/content/dam/Census/ library/visualizations/time-series/demo/families-and-households/hh-6.pdf

3   Kyle Barker, "STORE HOUSE: unpacking the American Dream," 2014, https://dspace. mit.edu/handle/1721.1/87138.

4   US Census Bureau, "Homeownership in the United States: 2005 to 2019," March 25, 2021, https://www.census.gov/newsroom/press-releases/2021/homeownership.html.

5   US Census Bureau, "Table 5. Homeownership Rates for the United States: 1964 to 2022," https://www.census.gov/housing/hvs/files/qtr122/tab5.xlsx.

6   Alicia VanOrman and Linda A. Jacobsen, "U.S. Household Composition Shifts as the Population Grows Older; More Young Adults Live With Parents," PRB, February 12, 2020, https://www.prb.org/resources/u-s-household-composition-shifts-as-the-population-grows-older-more-young-adults-live-with-parents/.

7   Statista, "Number of single-person households in the United States from 1960 to 2020," December 2020, https://www.statista.com/statistics/242022/number-of-single-person-households-in-the-us/.

8   S. Claire Conroy, "the 98 percent solution," Architect, May 7, 2007, https://www. architectmagazine.com/practice/the-98-percent-solution_o.

9   Ellen Dunham-Jones, "Seventy-Five Percent," *Harvard Design Magazine*, no. 12, http://www.harvarddesignmagazine.org/issues/12/seventy-five-percent.

10 US Census Bureau, "New Residential Construction," https://www.census.gov/ construction/nrc/index.html?CID=CBSM+EI.

11 Clare Trapasso, "Are 'Fixer Upper' Stars Chip and Joanna Gaines Saving Waco, or Destroying It?" Realtor.com, February 10, 2020, https://www.realtor.com/news/trends/ did-fixer-upper-stars-chip-and-joanna-gaines-save-or-destroy-waco/.

12 Louise McCready, "Form in Motion: Architect Zaha Hadid on Her Exhibit at the Philadelphia Museum of Art," Vogue, February 23, 2011, https://www.vogue.com/ article/form-in-motion-architect-zaha-hadid-on-her-exhibit-at-the-philadelphia-museum-of-art.